Courageous

HOW TO TRANSFORM PAIN INTO POWER

by Dr. Kathi Middleton

Courageous: How To Transform Pain Into Power
Copyright © 2020
ISBN: 978-0-578-78327-7

All rights reserved. In accordance with the U.S. Copyright Act of 1976, the scanning, uploading, and electronic sharing of any part of this book without the permission of the publisher constitutes unlawful piracy and theft of the author's intellectual property. If you would like to use material from the book (other than for review purposes), prior written permission must be obtained by contacting Dr. Kathi Middleton at www.kathimiddleton.com. Thank you for supporting the author's rights.

Contact the author:
www.kathimiddleton.com
All social media: @dr.kathimiddleton

Credits
Editorial: Carla DuPont
Cover Design: Richard Anthony Evans

In this compelling self-help, you will learn:

- How to release the pain of your history
- How to release limiting beliefs
- How to own your story
- How to learn yourself
- How to face your fears
- How to pace yourself for the journey ahead
- How to create a compelling vision
- How to build a healthy community
- How to commit to continuous growth

Your commitment to lifelong growth and sustainability is compiled in each chapter, undertaking each principle of *Courageous: How To Transform Pain Into Power.*

Courage is the most important of all the virtues, because without courage you can't practice any other virtue consistently. You can practice any virtue erratically, but nothing consistently without courage.

Maya Angelou

Dedication

This book is dedicated to those who are desperately seeking courage to rise beyond the pain of their past, embrace their present, and create a powerful life. I know what it feels like to be stuck, yet believe you were created to live a powerful life. Cheers to you for summoning the courage already inside of you!

Thank you all for your support, especially my Darling Daughter, Mom, Dad, family, friends, mentors, and Carla.

Introduction

A high school sophomore is sitting in the principal's office with her parents — for all the wrong reasons. This meeting is to inform her parents that she will be expelled from school. Sitting quietly, she watches her parents intently as they exasperatedly try to convince the principal that she is a straight-A student who deserves another chance. Unmoved, the principal, refuses to give her another chance because her record of fights and aggressive behavior can no longer be tolerated.

As they walk out of the school defeated, she thinks back to what has happened throughout her young life. None of the adults in the room asked her why she behaved the way she did or cared why she was always angry. Since her cries had been ignored, she acted out in hopes that someone would finally recognize her. She was not seen when she witnessed her parent's abusive marriage. She was not heard when she revealed being sexually abused by a relative. Her questions were ignored after finding out she was born in a mental hospital to a mother with schizophrenia and the mother and father who were raising her were not her biological parents.

After moving out on her own at the tender age of 16, she began searching for peace and expression. She thought she found the answers in her personal and professional accolades; however, divorce and a fore-closure rocked her to her very core. Blow after blow, a downward spiral made her question her very existence.

After many years of hardship and being on her own, her life shifted. One day, she saw a lady who embodied the success she so desperately desired. This lady represented a possibility of what life could look like despite the pain she had experienced. This moment sparked an act of newfound courage to create a better life.

Dr. Kathi Middleton has wanted to show up as the best version of herself for quite some time. Now, I am that version. I want to share the principles I believe will help you tap into the greatness that lives within you. I want to transparently share my life's story to help you find the courage to heal from your past, realize your full potential, and reach the dreams that may seem so far away. I will also share key takeaways from iconic people who were sources of inspiration along my journey to greatness. Each one of us is created with a unique greatness and purpose. Greatness is about us tapping into our God-given identity and gifts to make ourselves, and the world, better. There is no better time to be courageous and achieve greatness.

The time is now! Are you ready?

Contents

SECTION ONE: Reconcile Your Past
Chapter 1: Release the Pain of Your History 12
Chapter 2: Release Limiting Beliefs 31
Chapter 3: Own Your Story 44

SECTION TWO: Embrace the Present
Chapter 4: Learn Yourself 55
Chapter 5: Face Your Fears 71
Chapter 6: Pace Yourself for the Journey 80

SECTION THREE: Excited for the Future
Chapter 7: Create a Compelling Vision 94
Chapter 8: Build a Healthy Community 108
Chapter 9: Commit to Continuous Growth 117

Courageous

HOW TO TRANSFORM PAIN INTO POWER

SECTION ONE

Reconcile Your Past

1

Release the Pain of Your History

"If you do not make peace with your past, it will keep showing up in your present."

Dr. Wayne W. Dyer

"You know JoAnn is your momma, right?"

I can still hear these words from my ailing grandfather ringing loudly in my ear. I was just ten-years-old when he asked me. Was it a real question or a rhetorical one? Confused, I sat there wondering, *Why was he saying this to me*? My parents were Carolyn and Sonny. They raised me all my life with my siblings Christopher and Shamelle.

My grandfather was in his late 80s, and maybe he wasn't entirely in his right mind. How could JoAnn be my mom? I didn't know a lot about her. JoAnn was my aunt who suffered from schizophrenia and lived in a mental hospital. The only memory I had of JoAnn was searching for her at the family reunion that she ran away from. We spent the weekend looking for her, hoping she was okay. I remember feeling a unique sadness and worry that my cousins didn't share. I, however, didn't understand these strong feelings at the time.

I suppressed them and tucked this question from my grandfather away, secretly hoping there was no truth to it. I was only ten, but I had already experienced so much pain that didn't feel I had the strength to cope with another blow. My nights were tortured and sleepless as I wrestled with the reality that my innocence had already been robbed when my uncle molested me. It would be many years later before I would learn, understand, and heal from this realty and its effect on my emotions. Before I could heal, I had to find peace.

Seventeen Years Later...

Blasting Jay-Z, Maxwell, and Coldplay, I anticipated a typical commute. If I played the music loud enough, I could almost drown out the dreaded reality that I would be sitting in Atlanta's rush hour traffic for the next hour and a half. I wanted desperately to escape the guilty thoughts that I would likely be late picking up my daughter from aftercare, again! But this day was some-what atypical. I found myself in a daze, depressed and uneasy about my life. It wasn't just the daunting list of to-dos for the week or the never-ending fantasies about my future; I wasn't at peace with the reflection I saw in the rearview mirror. A young woman who felt overcome and overwhelmed by her life looked back at me. If there was a silver lining, I was oblivious to it. Confusion, unhappiness, and, most of all, defeat hung menacingly over my head. At 27-years-old, this did not feel like the prime of my life.

Everyone thinks they can handle anything and achieve everything in their late 20s! My friends and colleagues were busy creating their dream lives even if that meant spending most of their time being serial daters with aspirations for marriage and working countless hours to advance their careers. I, on the other hand, was busy pulling my life apart. I purchased my first home at the age of 20 and my dream home shortly after that, but the bank foreclosed on it by the time I was 25. That was around the same time of my divorce, after one year of marriage, and my resignation from the six-figure salary job I landed right out of college. While fantasizing about the white picket fence and the perfect smiling family, I was learning to cope with the challenges of being a single, young mother.

This chronic cycle of significant wins followed by dramatic failures, was devastating. To achieve and lose so much in such a short period of time let me know that I was doing something wrong and my gut said it was directly related to my tumultuous past. At this moment, I knew what I had to do. I needed to go back and confront the pain of my past to heal. Until I made peace with my story, I wouldn't be able to create or sustain a healthy future.

This is where my journey began and these are the steps I took to release the pain of my history.

Making Peace with my History
The first step was making the choice to release the pain of molestation and the betrayal of not being believed.

Molestation perverted my reality of the world, people, and most significantly, myself. Being molested at an early age left me in a state of confusion about my sexuality and caused me to have low self-esteem. But it was just as damaging that when I finally mustered up the courage to share that I was molested, my family swept it under the rug. This made my trust issues worse. My abuser had broken my trust and my confidantes had, too.

 I was suffering from arrested development. Arrested development is an abnormal state in which developmental progress has stopped prematurely. In my case, I was an almost 30-year-old woman in a fully developed body with the emotional wholeness of a 10-year-old girl. I was outraged and felt like my life would forever be scarred. I tried to validate holding on to this pain, but, holding on to the pain was scarier than releasing it. Holding on to the past was stopping me from developing into a happy, fulfilled, and peaceful version of myself. By expressing the pain I felt from being molested, I was able to mature from the hurt 10-year-old girl who felt hopeless to a woman who was committed to her growth. This allowed happiness and wholeness to emerge.

 In the second step, I chose to heal from the pain of discovering my adoption. Unexpectedly learning at the age of 12 that the people raising me were not my biological parents shook me to my core. What little foundation I had crumbled, and I built my life on these broken pieces. My adoptive parents, whom I have affectionately always referred to as Mom and Dad, loved me. I was extremely grateful they stepped in to raise me. However, learning that my aunt, who suffered from schizophrenia and was the black sheep of the family, was my birth mother was difficult. I tried to cope with this discovery, but I found myself angrily lashing out at anyone in sight.

For the third step, I discovered empathy in counseling. I was familiar with the terms sympathy and empathy; however, I used these terms interchangeably without considering the difference. Sympathy is when a person shares the same feelings as another person, often expressed when someone is grieving or has suffered a loss. In contrast, empathy is where a person imagines or understands how someone else may have felt. An empathic person puts themselves in another person's shoes without necessarily having those feelings. The bitterness and anger I felt from being lied to about my birth mother left me numb. I coped with my pain by ignoring it. As a result, I felt no empathy for others and didn't even have it for myself. Through the counseling process, I developed understanding and compassion for myself, my birth mother, and my parents. I realized everyone did the best they could to manage life's circumstances, including me. The discovery and practice of empathy began my healing process with adoption.

Lastly, I chose to heal from the pain of divorce. Divorce felt like my first major failure as an adult. I was continually seeking affirmation that I was good enough after being molested, while knowledge of my adoption left me feeling rejected and inadequate. For most of my life, I coped with my feelings by overperforming and over-achieving. I thought being married and raising a family would make me feel whole and worthy, but this fantasy was short-lived. We were young and naïve about what we were getting into and neither of us was prepared or committed to the process of marriage. Within just a year, our volatile union ended.

Counseling helped me to realize I was idolizing a fantasy, opposed to embracing my reality. My marriage was unhealthy and needed to end. It was okay that I didn't have the white picket fence fantasy. It was okay that I hadn't envisioned being a single mother. I recognized I had tried to heal from my parents' failed marriage by making my marriage work. I sincerely wanted my daughter to grow up in a home with her mother and father, even if that home was not happy because most of her friends had both parents at home. I needed to release the fantasy of what my family was supposed to look like, make peace with my divorce, and create a life that I loved. This acceptance of my past created a new excitement and zeal for my future.

Reflect on the hardships I just described to you. Think about your own life as it pertains to your relationships, family, or career. Is there any past hurt or pain that you need to release?

Being courageous requires a peaceful mind void of clutter and noise. Whether we realize it or not, reflecting on past mistakes and poor decisions can lead us to constant rehashing, which is what I did every single day before seeking help. The echoes of our past take up so much space that they push out the good. Then, instead of seeing any positive aspects that we should be learning from, we only focus on the damage. This type of negative behavior takes us further and further away from the brave mindset we need to accomplish greatness.

No one is immune from experiencing these echoes of the times. Sometimes we think we are on top of a situation and it all falls apart. Sometimes we feel that we did our best and still fall short. Sometimes unfavorable circumstances in life happen completely outside of our control. When losses are fresh, we amplify what didn't go the way we thought it should have. When hit with unexpected news, we look at how different life could have been, projecting only rosy, positive outcomes. Even when the result of the situation we are focused on was outside of our control, feelings of self-deprecation can be intense.

Why You Should Let Go

To create the new, you must be in the present. New relationships, friendships, and work opportunities require you to be attentive to the here and now. The present is calling you! It needs your attention. When we struggle to let go of a past that cannot be altered, we rob the present of the attention it deserves. If you hold on to a past incident where you were the victim and have regrets, then you are likely aware that holding on to the situation is also holding you back. You cannot go back in time to change what was done or said. You can only take responsibility for making a concerted effort to lead a more peaceful, more cheerful existence. Letting go will enable you to overcome challenges associated with the hardships you agonize over, but you will emerge a stronger, more accomplished version of yourself.

Another reason to let go of the past is that putting hardships behind you is to emotionally free yourself. Have you ever noticed that in movies, when a female character goes through a bad break-up, she does one of two things: changes her hair or cries while eating a carton of ice cream? Why do you think this is? Because art imitates life! It's common to want to do something drastic after a bad break-up to free ourselves and get into a new mindset. As you relish in the newness of the change, you are cultivating a new mindset for the present. Letting go of the past is much the same. By eliminating that old baggage you are carrying, you are freeing yourself to enjoy new experiences in a reclaimed future.

"Perspective makes all the difference. It's not what you look at; it's what you see."

Steve Maraboli

Things Could Have Gone Differently

Knowing that perspective is more about *how* you see than *what* you see can give you a different "perspective" on how to view your past. I am not telling you to let go of the past as if it did not exist; I am telling you to alter the way you see what you see. Acknowledge the pain and explore the new context for your experiences. What if I had stayed in my marriage and we ended up hurting one another? What if I hadn't been molested? I wouldn't have the capacity to be empathetic for others who have had similar experiences. Express the pain that you have, think about how life could have gone differently, think about the upside of your experiences and release yourself from the pain.

Your perspective alters your attitude. When I first learned I was adopted, I had a very negative outlook on it. The discovery was devastating to me. I felt discarded like my parents didn't want me. Expressing my emotions in counseling helped me to develop a positive view of being adopted to see that I was chosen. One of the beliefs that helped to shape my new mindset was when I realized as an adult that my childhood could have been drastically different. Despite circumstances, a great deal of my childhood was joyful. If I had not been adopted by my parents, my life could have gone down a treacherous path. I had to see my adoption as a blessing, one that could have protected me from unknown struggles. Changing my perspective on my past helped me to see that if I had grown up with my birth parents, they might not have been equipped to take care of me. I also accepted that although my reality was not without pain, it was perfect and purposeful. My history shaped and formed me into a woman who could face adversity with courage.

Embrace What Was

It took me many years and a great deal of effort to accept my family's history of mental illness, being adopted, molested, and divorced. Since there was nothing that I could have done differently, I had to let go of the negative feelings and embrace what was. The past was just that: the past. It couldn't be redone, rewound, or renegotiated. When making peace with our history, we must choose to embrace it and move forward versus replaying the infinite ways it could have gone differently. I finally accepted I wouldn't be the person I am today if things had been different.

Express the Pain

Acknowledging our emotions is one of the most helpful steps for releasing the past. It is impossible to heal from what you refuse to recognize. Writing in a journal when you experience moments of clarity or confusion is a powerful outlet. Speaking with a trusted friend who can provide a listening ear or constructive advice is also helpful. You may even find that speaking directly to the person who wronged you helps to free that emotion. Sometimes, however, this is neither possible nor appropriate. If speaking to the person is not going to lead to a positive path forward, do not do so. Instead try writing a letter and not sending it.

Feel the sadness, hurt, anger, bereavement, failure, or disappointment. Accept that you are human and that it is ok to experience and feel pain. It is crucial to maintain a balance that will allow you to express yourself without wallowing in negative emotions. Strategies to maintain this balance are discussed in the next section on Being Mindful of Your Thoughts.

Be Mindful of Your Thoughts

One way to immediately begin renewing your mindset is to practice mindfulness. The brain is the most powerful organ in our bodies. Experts estimate that it thinks between 60,000 – 80,000 thoughts a day. That's an average of 2,500 – 3,300 thoughts per hour. With the incredible power of our minds and thoughts we can create positive transformation or prolong debilitating pain.

At times, reliving the past can become an obsession. We can create an entire world built upon what could have been. We can spend countless moments reliving, reorganizing, and restrategizing. Asking never-ending questions like, *How else could things have gone? What else could I have said? How could my life have gone down a different path?* Revisiting the past and reflecting on our lives, if we are not careful, can spark obsession over past events. This is a poor habit that will not move you forward. Anything at all can transport you back to the time and place that upsets you — a song on the radio, a social media post, or seeing someone you haven't seen in a long while. I am certainly not expecting you to completely forget, but I do want you to frame the way you reflect, differently. To do that, you need to have a strategy to jolt you from thinking in regret, to thinking in appreciation. This will help you positively transform your negative thoughts.

An effective strategy is to be aware that when these thoughts occur, you need to instantly change your train of thought. Focus on the abundance in your current situation. Look around you for blessings. What do you experience each day that just a few months or years ago you were praying for? You can also combat negative thinking with affirmations for a hopeful future. For example, instead of thinking, "I hate that I was reckless and got fired. I don't know what I'm going to do," try, "I am going to focus on finding a job that I love, working in a field I am passionate about, with a boss and co-workers I enjoy."

Maybe losing your job was your fault, and every day you are without a job, you wish you hadn't done whatever it was that got you fired. Or, perhaps you feel wronged because you were fired for no fault of your own. The result is the same: you are without a job. Think about how counterproductive it is to relive your past work events over and over when you could be using that time to look for a new position.

Ultimately, when you are struggling with the emotions of the past, focusing on anything else can pose quite a challenge. It is hard to live in the present when your mind is caged by regret and feelings of misfortune. Just as I was able to change my mindset to one of acceptance and move forward, you too, can free yourself from the bondage of emotional pain.

Seeking Help

Initially, I began the process of healing alone; however, I discovered quickly I would need help. One day I was speaking with a colleague about a work challenge, and in casual conversation, she brought up that she had been seeing a counselor for a couple of years since her divorce. I was a little surprised; I respected her very much and didn't perceive her as someone who needed counseling. When I was growing up, counseling was taboo. It was only for mentally ill or unstable people. However, I was desperate. I asked my colleague if she would share her counselor's information with me. I would love to say I researched the best counselor for me based on specialty, race, background expertise; however, that was not my reality. I was desperate for help, and I took the first recommendation. Luckily for me, it worked out very well! Later in this chapter, I will share tips that I learned over time for selecting a suitable counselor.

Beginning counseling was a courageous step. I felt like I was putting my life in a stranger's hands and possibly opening Pandora's box. The first step of counseling was to share my reason for coming. I shared the three major issues that were plaguing me. First, being molested at the age of ten left me feeling marked and dirty. Second, learning I was adopted from a cousin at the age of 12 left me with feelings of resentment and abandonment. Lastly, the end of my marriage and the reality of raising my daughter alone felt like a defeat that I was unable to overcome.

Through my counselor's help, I was able to process and gain a new perspective on these circumstances. I was able to remove the negative lens I saw my life through and instead see those instances as learning experiences that brought value and wisdom to my life. Step-by-step, my counselor and I peeled back the layers to address my wounds of molestation, adoption, mental illness, and divorce. This process was neither easy nor quick. It required my full commitment to my healing, despite the pain and distress that surfaced. My counselor didn't give me answers to fix my life. She held the space for me to clear the noise, ideas, and beliefs that no longer resonated with my true identity.

Reflection... Oprah Winfrey

"Anybody who has been verbally abused or physically abused will spend a great deal of their life rebuilding their esteem," media mogul Oprah Winfrey said in an interview with David Letterman at Ball State University. She, too, was molested at a young age, raped by a family member, and taken advantage of by her uncle, cousin, and a family friend. The abuse began when she was nine and lasted until she was 14, when her mother finally cast her out of her house. After being turned away from a detention home, Winfrey was sent to live with her father. He took her in, not knowing that she was pregnant. Two weeks after birth, the baby died. Winfrey reflects on the experience as very painful; however, she and her father saw this as a second chance for her. Oprah made a courageous choice to process her pain and move forward to create a powerful future. It wasn't a fresh start, but if she could make peace with her past, she could move forward focused on her "here and now." Because Oprah processed her pain and did not sulk in it forever, she was able to move forward with her life.

Oprah went on to create and host The Oprah Winfrey Show, the highest-rated television program of its kind in history. It was nationally syndicated from 1986 to 2011. She was also the wealthiest African American of the 20th century and North America's first Black multi-billionaire. She has been ranked the greatest Black philanthropist in American history and among the most influential women in the world. Oprah epitomizes the power of releasing your past to create a powerful future.

What happened to me, what happened to Oprah Winfrey, and those things you may have experienced are part of our stories. It is embedded in the very fiber of our beings. Our past provides a foundation for our life and growth; how we cope with it determines how we heal, enjoy our present, and create our future. You are the totality of everything you have seen, heard, or experienced. Embracing your past is necessarily embracing your current self. It is impossible to live a courageous life full of greatness when your mind is in turmoil, and you lack self-love and acceptance of your life experiences. I challenge you to commit to the process of acknowledging, accepting, and releasing your past to embrace a peaceful present and create a powerful future.

Conclusion

Making peace with the past is easier said than done—take it from someone who has been through the process. With fortitude and my counselor's support, I was able to process and gain a new perspective for the circumstances of my past, differently. I was able to remove the negative lens I saw my life through and began to see those events as learning experiences that brought value to my life. Releasing my divorce and the fantasy of what my family was supposed to look like helped me to embrace being a single mom and dating. Acknowledging and releasing the pain of being molested allowed me to rebuild my confidence and self-esteem. Accepting the reality that I was adopted, and my birth mother suffered from a mental illness helped me gain a new perspective that I was chosen while embracing a journey of self-care.

I strongly suggest seeking counseling as part of your self-care regimen. Your life does not need to be in shambles to see a counselor. These are four steps you can take to find a suitable counselor:

1. Ask trusted friends and family members for recommendations.
2. Search online, including the following sites: www.psychologytoday.com, www.blacktherapistnetwork.com, www.faithfulcounseling.com.
3. View a counselor's photo to see and follow your intuition.
4. Book an initial appointment, ask questions, and be patient with the process.

Below is a list of the primary benefits I received from counseling:

- A greater sense of self-acceptance, self-esteem, and self-awareness to manage life changes, challenges, and decisions
- Improved communication and interpersonal skills
- Increased awareness and ability to express my needs, desires, and fears
- Better ability to confront and develop healthy habits and perspectives to persevere through depression, anxiety, and stress
- Enhanced relationship with self and others
- Improved confidence and self-belief

Actively and consistently seeking counseling throughout my 30s was a deliberate and necessary decision. Despite my apprehension and initial discomfort, I committed to the process. My counselor helped me to see the benefits of quieting my thoughts to enable the healing process. I needed to go back to that scared child, hear her voice, and feel her pain. Once I learned to have empathy for that child, I was able to have compassion for the young lady who wanted to grow and become resilient.

I had not coped or shown myself compassion, nor had I developed the skill of empathy. As an adult, I realized that my immediate reaction when someone was hurt, whether it was a friend or even my child, was "toughen up, get up, and cope!" Acknowledging the pain or providing a remedy to soothe the pain was not a part of the equation. I am still developing the skill of empathy; however, now that I am aware of the gap, I have created the opportunity to develop and apply more empathy. When empathy is applied to a situation, we are no longer seeking to make sense, change, or resolve the circum-stances of the situation. Empathy allows us to place ourselves in the situation to understand and accept the variables as they are. This process of empathy and acceptance creates a space of peace for us to embrace the present and to let go of the past.

No matter how much we might like to forget some of the poor decisions we experienced or contributed to in our pasts, those experiences mold who we become and what we want out of life. The perspective you create of your past will impact your future. Gaining a positive outlook and peace about my past has allowed me to develop a sensitivity for others who are adopted, molested, and divorced. There have been countless occasions where I have been able to provide a listening ear or share my personal story to encourage someone. While some life lessons leave us hurt and wounded, other experiences teach us appreciation and how to lead happier lives. We create some of these experiences, while others are out of our control.

Exercise: Create a List of Items to Release from Your Past

Close your eyes and for five minutes imagine yourself fully embracing the fullness of everything you are and desire to become. Now open your eyes and make a list of every painful experience that you will need to let go of to create a courageous new possibility. I encourage you to take this list and begin working with a trusted professional or counselor to release your past.

2

Release Limiting Beliefs

"We learn our belief systems as very little children, and then we move through life creating experiences to match our beliefs. Look back in your own life and notice how often you have gone through the same experience."

Dr. Wayne W. Dyer

Most of the beliefs we hold are created as children. To each of us, our beliefs are truths that we hold to navigate this world. If we believe something or someone is beautiful, ugly, right, wrong, or impossible, that is what it is to us. Limiting beliefs are the views we have that keep us from reaching our potential. In addition to releasing painful experiences, to empower myself, I had to release limiting beliefs. We are all a product of our experiences until we decide to create something more compelling. Yet, it is essential to acknowledge that those experiences have molded and guided us. Your upbringing, education, and adult experiences impact how you view yourself, abilities, different races and cultures, love, money, politics, relationships, and religion.

Beliefs, which affect how we see ourselves and others, are usually formed in two ways. They can take shape empirically, through our own experiences and deductions, or didactically, accepting what we have been taught. I distinctly remember my younger cousin telling me, "I'm never going to be rich because nobody in my family has ever been rich." Sadly, that type of limiting belief is paralyzing. There were moments in my career where I felt isolated, confined, and targeted based on my parents' experiences with segregation in the '50s and racism in the early '90s. Granted, racism still exists today; however, your perception and ability to process it is impacted mainly by your belief system. Releasing limiting beliefs has empowered me to move forward past the stifling effects of racism.

"Race is the least reliable information you can have about someone. It's real information, but it tells you next to nothing."

Toni Morrison

I felt that because of the color of my skin, I would be trapped under a glass ceiling. My parents spent most of their formative years growing up in the South, experiencing segregation. Brown v. The Board of Education happened halfway through their primary schooling. Many of their experiences were separate and certainly not equal. They saw and experienced, first-hand, how Blacks were mistreated in comparison to whites.

    I formed my beliefs about race when I was a young child. I remember my father telling me about the discrimination he encountered during and after fighting for his country in the Vietnam War. Throughout his time of service, Black men were delayed in receiving rank compared to their white counterparts based on skin color alone. He returned home from serving his country in the early 1970's. On one occasion, he traveled from Ohio to Atlanta after visiting family and attempted to have dinner at the Greyhound bus station. He was denied service at a restaurant that was "White Only" and was forced to patronize a "Colored Only" restaurant. These moments were humiliating and debilitating. Despite these injustices, my father still did his best to teach his children to treat everyone equally.

    In contrast, my mother worked in corporate America and faced a significant amount of racism there. I recall her coming home and venting about the inequalities she faced as a minority manager and how it was challenging to be treated fairly and with the same respect as her white counterparts. In March of 1961, Pres. John F. Kennedy signed an executive order requiring government contractors to "take affirmative action" to build fair employment practices as a path to create a nation with nondiscrimination goals. Even though the system was designed to encourage employers to hire employees based on their credentials, minorities hired under Affirmative Action were subject to discrimination and being ostracized inside of the workplace. While my mother may have benefitted from Affirmative Action, she was still mistreated by many of her co-workers and superiors. Being in a room where she was the only brown or female face, her ideas were often drowned out and her authority was undermined because of the color of her skin.

Twenty years after watching my mother's reaction to workplace bias, I found myself facing comparable challenges. Forty years past The Civil Rights Act of 1964, there was still a vast disparity between the number of whites and minorities in the corporate workplace. Unconscious bias and discrimination remained prevalent at many organizations, and on occasion, I had a front-row seat to it. In moments, the inequalities felt overwhelming and undefeatable. However, I knew that to live courageously and take hold of every opportunity I desired, I had to create a new reality for myself despite any circumstances or limitations.

Another area, where I experienced limiting beliefs was being a single mom. For several years after my divorce, I struggled with my new normal of raising my daughter in a single parent home. These beliefs ran rampant in my subconscious mind and limited how I parented, managed my career, and dated. Of course, your responsibilities as a parent influence your choices; however, they should not limit the opportunities you see for yourself. I became more accepting of my new family dynamic as I began to envision a powerful future for myself and daughter. I also surrounded myself with successful and supporting single women who encouraged me to accomplish big goals. We will discuss more about building Healthy Community later in the book.

Limiting beliefs are self-imposed interferences we enact on ourselves that prevent us from accomplishing our goals. Regardless of how factual or illogical they may be, limiting beliefs convince us not to take action. They stem from opinions that seem very real to us, giving us a reason to latch on to the fear of moving forward. For example, my mother's experience with racism in corporate America doesn't have to dictate the value I carry for myself with my current situation in corporate America.

In the blog, "7 False Beliefs That Are Holding You Back in Life" Lifehack.org encourages you to question whether you have said the following to yourself:

- "I can't tell the truth because I may get judged…"
- "I don't want to get close to this person lest my heart gets broken…"
- "I don't want to ask for what I want because, what if I get rejected?"
- "I can't trust people because I've been betrayed before…"
- "I can't pursue my dreams because I don't know what I'd do if I fail…"
- "I can't do X because of Y…"

- "I can't do A because of B…"

Examine Your Life for Limiting Beliefs

Throughout life, you may have found that it is easier to believe in something negative or limiting. Before you determine how something affects you, you must first determine what is affecting you. Identification is the key. How can you identify limiting beliefs? Begin by making a list of the areas of your life that are the most displeasing to you. What do you deal with or go through regularly that brings you anxiety or unhappiness that you are not actively making strides to adjust? If you would rather struggle through it than make changes to modify how the situation affects you, more than likely, there is a limiting belief there.

There are several general areas where unhappiness can reside in our day-to-day lives. Think finances. Is your income what you desire it to be? Are you financially free enough to obtain your needs and wants? Are you equipped to give yourself the experiences you desire? Is your savings account comfortable enough to make you proud? Think of your health. Are you pleased with your weight and appearance? Are you comfortable with the way clothes fit? Do you schedule routine doctors' appointments? Think relationships. Are your relationships fulfilling? Are you satisfied with your social life personally, socially, and at work? If the answer to any of these questions is "no" and you are not doing anything to change your current situation, there is a limiting belief keeping you stagnant.

After you have identified where the unhappiness lies, think about what beliefs you have that make the change so difficult. Don't focus on whether the reasons have merit or not, just write down what they are. Do you say any of the following things to yourself?

- I'll never have enough money to get the house I want.
- I'll always be in debt.
- I don't make enough money to travel.
- If I get a lot of money people will say I've changed.
- People will steal from me if I make a lot of money.
- Rich people act stuck up.

These beliefs about being financially free or having an abundance of wealth stem from deeply rooted feelings about money or the lack thereof. If you don't have "enough" and you want more, you should do what is necessary to acquire more. However, if you have never had "enough" money or "enough" of anything, you may be afraid that once you get it, it will somehow be taken away from you. This same method of thinking can be applied to relationships, career moves, or any other avenue of your life.

Acknowledge that these are beliefs, not truths!
No matter how false something is, if you believe it, it is real to you! That reality will make you adjust your life around it. Have you ever heard of "The Glass Delusion"? It was a disorder that emerged between the 15th and 17th

centuries where people felt they were made of glass. The psychiatric disorder swept through Europe, causing people to go out of their way to rearrange their lives so they would not shatter. One gentleman used the bathroom standing up because he thought sitting down would make his posterior shatter. King Charles IV had his clothes made with special reinforcements and avoided letting people touch him so he would not shatter. Now, we know this is ridiculous because we simply could not live if we were made of glass. With all of the hugging, hand-shaking, falling down, and horse-play, we would shatter into millions of pieces making life impossible.

The limiting beliefs that keep us pigeon-holed are much like "The Glass Delusion" in that they are beliefs, not truths. We perceive them to be mountains in the way of accomplishing our goals. We treat them as rules that govern our lives, never questioning their validity. Merriam-Webster defines a belief as something that is accepted, considered to be accurate, or held as an opinion, while the truth is defined as the body of real things, events, and facts. Beliefs do not require evidence, merely faith in them. Truths cannot be argued; they can be verified as certain.

Acknowledge that the beliefs you are holding, probably since childhood, may not be real. They are not big, bad, scary monsters hiding under the bed of success. Be honest with yourself regarding why your finances, your weight, and your stagnancy at work are where they are. The only fact about it all is, the only thing holding you back is you!

Try on a Different Belief

Since the beliefs we maintain influence our lives and impact our decisions, why not believe something positive? Transforming our mindsets requires us to welcome new perspectives and be open to possibilities. This is what change is all about. We must choose the desired outcome. What is it that we'd like to have, do, see, or become? We must confirm which limiting belief is keeping us from achieving the fantasy ideal we see in our minds. Then we must challenge that belief. Why have those beliefs been so real to us? Where did they come from? What about my life disproves this belief? How has the opposite of what I believed worked for others?

Once we do the work to see where limiting beliefs stem from and precisely what mindset is behind them, we can do different, more transformative types of work. Only having an awareness of our limiting beliefs is not enough to change those types of thoughts about how they impact us. Sadly, acknowledging the limit in our thought processes is where a lot of people stop. By this juncture in life, there is an elevated amount of emotion invested, it's almost as if a physical barrier of change has been created. The deeper the conviction, the harder it will be to adjust the feelings and mindset behind it.

Take Different Action

We can empower ourselves by adopting new beliefs. New beliefs must be believable, that is the leading principle in selecting them. If new beliefs are not plausible, our minds will not be retrained, thus leaving us in the exact same situation we are currently in. Consider who you wish to become and what you want to achieve, then frame your belief around the better, more elevated version of yourself.

We can train our minds to see the benefits of transformed beliefs. The more benefits, the greater the motivation and transformative power we have to fuel the change of old patterns and behaviors. Additionally, finding ways to strengthen new beliefs will make them more plausible and more likely to stick to us. Our new mindset can be reinforced by pictures or symbols on our screensavers, changing passwords to a keyword or phrase, or creating action behind it. We need references and remembrances. References of others who we've seen embody the change we seek; recollections of a slogan or mantra for us to recite to ourselves. The more references and remembrances we capture, the stronger our faith is that we can live up to the belief that we have put in place for ourselves.

We are greater than our fears. Limiting beliefs and bias are very real; however, they only have as much power as we give them. Our situations will never change unless we invoke that change. Our world around us will continue to be as suffocating and stagnant as we allow it to be. We are greater than stagnation, more powerful than self-imposed limits. Why? Because we are living courageously beyond any doubt that we have had in the past. If there's ever a time when you need a nudge of, "Yes I can," think Barack Obama.

Reflection... Barack Obama

"There's a great presumption of dangerousness for Black men," Former President Barack Obama said. What was your impression upon seeing Obama was a viable candidate at the Democratic National Convention? Did you laugh? Did you automatically exclude him as having a real chance? Or were you hoping for change? Now, if you did not think he'd have a chance, ask yourself why not?

Obama has quite arguably overcome the largest gap in racial bias in modern history. To become the first Black President of the United States of America was no small feat. After 220 years of white presidents, the people of the country chose him. He was built for the journey, having experienced racial bias nearly from birth. He was not born into wealth, a pedigreed education, or influence. His path was much different than the paths other presidents took. Limiting beliefs could have taken their toll, preventing him from soaring at any point.

Born to a mother from Wichita, Kansas and a father from Kenya, Obama experienced racial bias as a biracial child in the 60s and 70s from birth. The maternal grandparents who raised him were proud of the public servant values they instilled in him. He used scholarships and student loans to pay for college. He worked to help rebuild marginalized communities in Chicago devastated by the closure of local steel plants. He found the work gratifying and nurtured the notion of bringing everyday people and politics together to seek change.

Before running for any public office, he was named the first Black President of the Harvard Law Review. That experience alone began to prepare him for the types of racial bias he would face as his gaze fell on the White House.

He could have easily told himself that America would never vote for him to be president as a Black man, or he shouldn't have children because he grew up without a father. Had those limiting beliefs founded in his childhood, by never having seen a Black president or having a relationship with his father, taken flight, the history of a nation would have been altered. Regardless of how the "negative" aspects of his background were perceived by himself or others, he was determined not to be a product of what he had experienced. Racial bias can and does lead to limiting beliefs. Thankfully, Obama was able to keep any external or internal murmurings from deterring him from achieving his goals.

Conclusion

Remember, you can create a powerful life absent from bias and limiting beliefs. This requires intentionality and an open mind. Former President Obama did not allow limiting beliefs of his working-class family to keep him from applying to Harvard, no more than the color of his skin kept him out of the presidential race. Do not allow statistics to dictate your future. According to the American Council on Education, only 12% of GED diploma holders are likely to complete a postsecondary program within six years of passing the equivalency exam. Still, you can be in that 12%. Fifty percent of small businesses fail by their fifth year, but you can be in the 50% that succeed. Roughly 67% of second marriages fail, but your marriage can be the 33% that make it. Eliminating limiting beliefs is a tremendous step in reaching any level of success you may have.

Limiting beliefs are not something we have to have. No rule says we must subscribe to limiting beliefs, or we must pass them down to our children. Once we figure out which limiting beliefs are holding us back, we can catapult ourselves into greatness by eliminating them.

3

Own Your Story

"Owning your story is the bravest thing you will ever do."

Brené Brown

I tapped into a new power when I owned my story. We each have chapters of our life that we may find more challenging to open than others. This is because we are programmed to avoid pain, so the parts of our story that conjure up unpleasant memories are often cast to the far corners of our minds. Embarrassment and shame make you more prone to hide it than let it be known.

I have a complete grasp of that train of thought. Through my journey, I have been on a constant mission to be better, have better, and do better. I wanted to create a lasting marriage, achieve the pinnacle of success in my education and work, and make my daughter always feel understood. I didn't feel like I was hiding my story, but I didn't feel compelled to share it either. The last thing I wanted was to dredge up old emotions that would wear me down instead of helping me to keep my momentum. I'd cover up my failures, create a new goal for myself and work towards that goal without looking back.

That is until I realized the power of owning my story. Observing the parallels between my mother and me in our corporate America landscapes, though 20 years apart, helped me to see that my past molded who I am. I would not be the driven, motivated version of myself without having to overcome the adversities in my path. I could no longer cast it aside or hide it if I wanted to live authentically. I began to intentionally show up in the world as my authentic self, scars, bruises, and all. This new way of being was invigorating and, to my surprise, inspiring. When I shared my past and present truths, people were touched, moved, and inspired to live their lives more courageously as well.

In the summer of 2019, I taught a technology course at a local university in Atlanta, Georgia. My students were inspired to dream big and aspired to technology careers that previously seemed out of their reach. During my time of teaching, I was asked to perform a TedTalk hosted by the college. I was excited about the opportunity and looked forward to informing and inspiring students on a larger scale about the Power of Technology. During the first rehearsal, it became evident, I wouldn't be able to just share theories and statistics, the audience needed to know me! Not the Ph.D., highly successful career woman and doting mother. They needed to understand the abused, rebellious, and confused young girl who was expelled from high school and would eventually persevere through every obstacle and leverage technology to create a powerful life.

I thought I was delivering a TedTalk to help others; however, this experience helped me as much as anyone. The process allowed me to be honest with who I was without reservation. I didn't sprinkle small parts of my story here and there or tailor it for a specific audience as I had in the past, or cower away from my truths. I let it all hang out because I wanted my story to encourage others who had experienced similar struggles.

Taking such a giant leap from suppression to sharing on a national stage was daunting. I was determined. Every time I thought about how I would be perceived after friends, acquaintances, and colleagues found out about my past, I got physically ill. Trepidation pulsed through my body with every beat of my heart. I experienced many sleepless nights, over-analyzed every detail of my story and even considered watering down my truth to make it more palatable. However, the more I prayed about sharing my story on a TedTalk and the people who would be helped, the more at peace I became. This was going to be a win for me, as well as those who had shared similar fates, but first, I had to truly own my story before I could share it.

Accepting Circumstances

Accepting circumstances means that you acknowledge the reality of your situation. Accept who you are, what you are, and what your life looks like. Even if your realistic view is horrible, before you can improve it, you must acknowledge it. You can powerfully create a new life for yourself once you view your picture honestly.

A few ways to accept circumstance are:

Own every outcome. Work to own every part of your current reality. Don't cower away from failures, instead look for lessons, not just successes. If the outcome is good, celebrate it; if it's undesirable, be honest about your part and how you can avoid making that same mistake next time.

Find your strength. No matter where you are, only you have the power to change it. Once you make up your mind to elevate your position, that is what will happen when you come up with a plan, then execute that plan. Be strong enough to realize that you control your reality.

Accept that struggles will come. The term "over-night success" didn't come from nowhere. It derived from people seemingly catapulting to success overnight. One day we could pass them on the street not knowing who they were, and the next day, they were a household name. Usually, those people have put in years of struggle and overcoming obstacle after obstacle to make it to the cover of magazines. You know the struggle is a part of the process. Roll with it choosing to make smart decisions to adjust your path rather than just flow with it.

Make Things Worse with Bad Choices/Self-sabotage

Self-sabotage occurs when you are on the cusp of getting something you really want, then you do something that undermines your efforts. Those who self-sabotage usually do not realize their words or actions are harming themselves. Instead, they blame outside forces as the reasons for their shortcomings. Let's say there is a major project coming up that you need to finish. Instead of working on the project, you self-sabotage by continually clicking refresh on your email inbox, looming on social media and doing smaller, menial tasks unrelated to the job at hand. When the project isn't done in the end, you may say you were busy or didn't have time when in actuality, you sabotaged yourself by deflecting your energy.

There are countless reasons why we self-sabotage including thinking patterns, intimacy issues, and unresolved fears. Self-sabotage is not a blanket occurrence. Look at your behaviors and time management skills to see if self-sabotage is an obstacle you need to overcome. The solution may be easier than you think once you work to understand the root of the issue.

Pain and Fear Leave You Stagnant

Perhaps you aren't making things worse, but if you aren't making them better either, then you are stuck.

I am very comfortable with a routine and a plan. Even if my routine is interrupted, I feel safe if I have a plan written out where I can see my goals and a way to achieve them. Fear of not knowing what lies ahead can cripple me into not moving, or it did until I learned how to live courageously.

If you sense that you are living below your potential, you could be. Why is that? Do you know what could be holding you back? Stagnation or procrastination is a sign that something deeper is afoot. You can beat yourself up about being still, but that won't cause you to move forward without getting to the root of the issue.

Quite possibly, pain or fear holds you back. Pain could stem from a past failure, where you didn't teach yourself to view the outcome as a stepping stone for growth. Pain could also linger after being let down by from someone you thought of very highly and you couldn't get past it.

Fear of failure can be equally debilitating. If you allow the fear you feel to manifest and persist, anxiety and hesitation begin to feel normal. In this case fear is not simply the usual caution, but an overwhelming feeling keeps you from creating, growing, being, and enjoying a new peak of life. Decide that fear is not an option, then kickstart the process to overcome what is holding you hostage from a fruitful and plentiful life.

Create by Transforming Pain into Power

When we begin to feel pain, we impulsively try to thwart it. As young children, we are told not to be sad. Once we get a little older, we pick up on cultural cues that teach us to avoid or minimize discomfort on all levels. Rather than feel emotional pain, we turn to alcohol, gambling, sex, drugs, and poor spending – anything to turn our attention away from what has put us in a stupor. We fight to mask the hurt, not realizing that it is more damaging than experiencing the pain to begin with.

You cannot be selective in choosing which emotions to numb. If you get into the practice of numbing sadness and heartbreak, it will be difficult to ever openly revel in happiness and joy. Even though we have such a wide range of emotions, the less you feel of one, the less you will feel of them all.

Challenge your perspective to find positivity. For example, the loss of a loved one can leave you devastated. Feel the sadness and emptiness, then focus on the positive impact they had on your life and the lives of others. If they were older, think about how full their life was and how much they were able to accomplish. Recall the quick-witted humor they had or a memorable moment the two of you had and hold it in the forefront of your heart instead of the emptiness left in their absence. Perspective plays a crucial role in turning negatives into positives.

Then do something powerful! Find a way to harness the energy you feel regarding your loss. This is much easier said than done, and no, it will not happen with the snap of a finger. But it can be done. The pain-to-power process can be a stepping stone to growth. Regarding the death of a loved one, perhaps this would be a great time to hold a memorial for others to share only positive and/or funny stories about your loved one. Maybe you'll be moved to start a scholarship in their honor.

When you allow yourself the freedom to envision the endless possibilities that power can bring you, creativity will also follow suit. Start a blog. Write a book. Gather neighbors to launch a garden in your community. Find a creative, powerful outlet for the pain to turn into something useful. You will be amazed at the trans-formation in yourself after such a positive drive shows you strength and tenacity you didn't even know you had.

Reflection... J.K. Rowling

When I think of managing obstacles, prominent author J.K. Rowling immediately comes to mind. Even if you have never read one of her international best-selling books turned international box office hits, her name should ring familiar. Growing up, Rowling was surrounded by books to the point where she landed fines for overdue books at her university's library. It wasn't until after her divorce, with an infant daughter on her hip, that she began weaving together the traces of *Harry Potter and the Philosopher's Stone*, that she'd spent five years jotting down notes and planning out plots of. Talk about turning pain into power.

Armed with only three completed chapters, she began soliciting literary agents. Only one responded that they wanted to hear more. It would take another five years before the book was completed and available in print. Seven more books would come, each one increasingly more successful than the last until, in 2001, the film adaptation of the first book was released by Warner Brothers.

Consider this, the creator of the bewitching world of Harry Potter lived a far from comfortable life before her books became all the rage across the world. Struggling as a single mother raising her child in absolute poverty, Rowling was living on government welfare when she wrote her first Harry Potter book. Today, she is one of the richest women in the UK. Are you overcome by the notion that "If she can do it, I can do it too?"

Not convinced yet? Think about the determination it took to climb the mountains of pain and frustration she felt all at once. After suffering a divorce and relocating to raise her daughter alone, Rowling harnessed her energy to create something positive. We don't know how she envisioned the Harry Potter series. However, do you think she ever imagined the acclaimed success that she has reached? She was able to get beyond her obstacles of having to work a job during the day and write only at night after her daughter went to sleep. Not only was she able to make her stamp in history but bring joy to the masses through her heartfelt imagination.

Conclusion

What are you facing that is blocking your J. K. Rowling level successes? What is keeping you from writing your book, launching your business, starting your foundation, or getting a promotion at your job? Who or what have you given the power to sabotage you? If it is someone else, eliminate the hold – and authority – that you have given them. If it is you, be honest with yourself about your past, your pain, and your fears.

Only you can control your narrative. Managing obstacles is not easy, but you are not alone. We all have hindrances in our lives that make it challenging to elevate from one level to the next. I am cheerleading you to go up just one level. Just one! Feel that success, let that feeling radiate through you, share it with loved ones or those you are connected to on social media. Then let it propel you to up the ante two more levels. Let small progress fuel your drive to reach the ultimate goals you have in life, whether it be genuine happiness or running for congress. You can do it!

SECTION TWO

Embrace the Present

4

Learn Yourself

"Knowing yourself is the beginning of all wisdom."

Aristotle

Learning myself was the most powerful decision I ever made. In my mid-twenties, before I discovered this, I had achieved a great deal of professional success. I was at the top of my career; I had just been promoted to a director at a Fortune 50 company. Yet, what should have been a peak moment in my career was intensely stressful.

I experienced extreme levels of pressure and a lack of support from my manager, the vice president of the department, daily. The department executives constantly bombarded me with requests while I facilitated intense high-stakes meetings that significantly impacted the company.

At my breaking point, I phoned a mentor in California. He had been my mentor for a few years and always provided sound wisdom. I shared my truth. I was in a highly visible role under a substantial amount of pressure to execute demanding decisions that I felt ill-prepared to make. Furthermore, my manager's unwillingness to confirm my decisions left me feeling vulnerable and unsupported.

After I shared the details and pled my case, I sat on the phone, waiting for my mentor to agree that the situation was unreasonable. Instead, to my surprise, he asked me a question that would change the trajectory of my career and, ultimately, life.

He asked, "Kathi, are you open to some coaching?"

I had never been asked if I was open to *anything*. I was so used to people just rattling off their advice. I answered with excitement, "Yes!"

He said, "What if your manager is confident in your abilities and that's why he's not reviewing the information with you beforehand?"

Suddenly, tears welled up in my eyes, and I cried uncontrollably. Before this moment, it *never* occurred to me, not one time, that my manager felt I was competent. Me, totally capable? Why wouldn't he have felt I was capable? I had the experience, I'd been working successfully in the role, and I'd proven myself which is why I had been promoted. However, those rational thoughts were not the thoughts that came to my mind during my frustration. Subconsciously my mind was filled with all the things I had experienced in my past: dishonesty, abandonment, not feeling good enough, and feeling like people were out to hurt me.

After I listened to my mentor's perspective, he invited me to participate in a personal development program to better understand myself and how my life's experiences impacted the way I showed up in the world. This program would change my life. It initiated the process of self-discovery, transforming the way I saw, understood, and experienced myself and others. Through personal and professional growth, training, and development, I was able to shift from focusing on accomplishments to tapping into greatness. I gained insight into myself and how my past experiences shaped the view from which I saw and experienced the world. I learned the breadth and depth of myself. I finally understood the intricacies and overarching themes that surrounded my life. Ultimately, I realized there was so much that I needed to learn about myself.

One of the most courageous things a person can do in their lifetime is to learn themselves. To begin this process, I set out on a quest to discover my history, personality, values, likes, dislikes, mindset, triggers, and aspirations.

Learning My History

As I mentioned earlier, making peace with the past was the first step of my journey. With my counselor's guidance, I embarked on a journey of revisiting my past. The counseling process was not easy; however, each step that I conquered made me stronger and wiser. For instance, I learned that the feelings surrounding my divorce really stemmed from ideologies of keeping my family together, achieving something my parents could not, even if it meant we were not happy. Learning about my adoption diminished my self-esteem, and suffering through molestation led to trust issues. Once I learned and release those things, I made room for growth and getting to know the real Kathi.

Discovering My Personality

Letting others down was a massive obstacle to learning who I was. I quickly became fixated on how I was perceived, which resulted in people-pleasing and struggling to weed through false affections. My focus was more on being viewed in a positive light than being true to myself. Most people don't like disappointing others, but rarely do they live their lives for the sole purpose of pleasing others. I had to consider how my decisions were influencing my life. I learned to stop allowing my presumed failures, disappointments, and indecisive mentality to guide my life. I learned to let my knowledge of truth free me to be courageous enough to reach for greater potential. It is through life's disenchantments I got to see the type of fire I was forged from, I learned what I was made of and what drove me.

Taking the time to get to know myself and set parameters for what I was willing to accept and not accept allowed me to move forward productively. I also underestimated how powerful knowing who I was, affected the road ahead. Instead of seeking permission from others about what I needed to do, I began to trust myself. This knowledge alleviated the disappointment and angst caused by making decisions that pleased others but were not true to my core needs.

Consider taking a personality assessment to better understand your unique persona. Several years ago, I completed the Myers-Briggs Personality Test and gained invaluable insight into my identity and patterns. The Myers-Briggs Personality Test is one of the most popular assessments used in the business world. However, the benefits carry over to all facets of your life. The goal of the test is to indicate your psychological preferences to evaluate and further understand yourself. For example, I was able to identify my tendency to make decisions based on subjective feelings versus objective information and logic. Gaining this awareness allowed me the ability to create habits to recognize this behavior and make an alternate choice. This doesn't mean I completely stopped applying "feels" to my decision making. This did allow me to apply them more objectively, which in turn, resulted in making more sound business and personal decisions.

Identifying My Core Values

For a long time, I lived without a set of guiding core values, otherwise known as fundamental beliefs. When I identified my core values, I asked myself the following questions. How do I want people to remember me? What do I want my life to represent? What values are essential to my life? What annoys me about others? What makes me feel strong? My core values include faith, authenticity, self-respect, love for others, and life-long learning.

I couldn't just think my way into becoming myself. I needed to embrace my mistakes and failures to discover my true identity. Discovering my true self required me to make peace and honor my experiences and journey. The lack of self-awareness can stem from insurmountable pain or life-altering experiences. I began to place a higher value on the time spent building my relationship with God and lean on His guidance. I had to be honest with myself to understand that my love for others should not keep me from expressing my true feelings or place their thoughts and opinions ahead of my own. In order to grow, I had to be okay with creating anew. I wanted to grow as a person, as a mother, and as a professional, which meant that I would constantly be learning for the rest of my life. There is tremendous beauty in knowing I am an original, which is something I now believe.

There is a great deal of power behind being secure in your own skin. Finding out who you are, does not come easily, and usually does not happen at a tender age. Asking yourself the question, "Who am I?" is often closely followed by, "What do I want to do and become?"

Determining My Aspirations

Simply put, there is a lot to lose by not learning yourself. Our performance, in any circumstance, is often based on what we aspire to at that moment. Think about a time where you asked to do something you were very excited about. For example, you were eager to deliver a presentation at work. At the end of the presentation, you received a standing ovation, and everyone commended your efforts. Now, think of a time when you were asked to do something you had trepidation about. For example, you were reluctantly volunteered to compete in a dance-off at work and your performance was lackluster. Often our performance is based on our abilities and approach to a situation.

What you *can* do versus what you *choose* to do should be based on your aspirations, which is why learning who you are is so important. When you are flowing in your ambitions, thoughts, and concepts come easily, your demeanor and attitude are enjoyable. Not knowing yourself well enough to decide what is best for you could lead to a great deal of dissatisfaction or grave consequences.

Gaining Awareness to Your feelings

What determines how you feel? Is it determined by how other people treat you? What's going on in the economy? The health of your children? Your job titles? It really should not be any of these things. No matter what is going on around you, you are in control of how you feel. My mother used to remind me that I am a thermostat, not a thermometer – I determine how my environment feels. If you don't feel like you are in control of your life, I challenge you to get to know yourself to figure out how to regain it.

Learning that you are in control of your feelings, brings self-awareness to an incredible new level. Learning to manage your mental state brings a new level of responsibility; however, not managing your mental state can be detrimental. Consider the lives of Whitney Houston, Amy Winehouse, and Michael Jackson. All three of these people were widely successful by anyone's standards. They were uniquely talented and had families that loved them and millions of fans who supported their work. Something else they each have in common is death by overdosing on drugs. Even through their wins, they did not know themselves well enough to control their mental state. Instead, they used drugs to alter their mental states so they would feel better.

Only we are in control of managing our feelings and minds to keep the outside world and our current circumstances from changing who we are. This is not to say things won't happen to you or around you that introduce negative feelings. With courage and resolve, you can take hold of these emotions and view your life positively.

A Positive Mindset

Having a positive mindset is maintaining an outlook that promotes favorable results. It is a mental state that fosters happiness, joy, health, and success, no matter what the situation. Your subconscious mind has power in controlling your life experiences — from the types of food you eat to the actions you take each day, the amount of income you earn, and even how you react to stressful situations.

Life will show up for you according to the point-of-view that you usually maintain. Not only do you look at any circumstance with a positive light, but you can take that positive light to the next level. The terms of success mean different things to different people. While for some success is described as having a spouse and two healthy, happy children, for someone else it may mean owning a billion-dollar business. One level of success for me was writing this book to help others live courageously.

Having the life you want begins with under-standing what is keeping you from having the life that you want and making the shifts necessary to eliminate those deterrents. There may be a lack of strategy, which simply means you should develop a plan. However, there are usually psychological components that hold us back, such as the fear of failure. With a positive attitude, you can have all that you want. If you believe life is full of good things just for you, you will see those things with your eyes, mind, and heart. Life is enjoyable. There are many things available to enjoy in life, such as good people, experiences, food, material things, and nature. You will have the courage to do the impossible, to go out there to achieve or obtain whatever it is that you want. A positive attitude is one of the most powerful secrets of success in business or life. Many successful people have said many times that success mostly depends 99% on our attitude and only about 1% on the skills for every individual in any endeavor. There is no replacement for hard work, but hard work alone won't get the job done.

Learning Your Emotional Triggers

Have you ever noticed how specific topics or instances evoke an unpleasant emotional response? The response may be guilt, sadness, anger, or envy. These responses are emotional triggers and we all have them. Emotional triggers make us uncomfortable and, in a way, convey that we are not living up to our full or even half-full potential. They have a way of potentially telling us which aspects of our lives are not pleasing to us or where we are the most frustrated.

Being able to identify what is bothersome to us helps us to protect that space, thus protecting our mental health. There is no way to avoid all the circumstances that emotionally trigger us, but by identifying what they are, we can put a plan into place that will help to lessen the blow.

I once had a close friend, Jasmine, who grew up in a home where her parents were highly critical, and her mother was quick-tempered, getting upset over any and everything. She was active in cheerleading and gymnastics and excelled in school, but if she was not number one, or did not receive straight A's, her parents belittled her because of it. All while growing up, she fought for their approval, which was often hard-won. As an adult, Jasmine's trigger was disapproval. She would bend over backwards not to upset others or make them mad at her because it would lead to feelings of isolation and pain from childhood. This is a good instance of how not knowing yourself leads to self-detriment.

You must identify your emotional triggers before you can heal from them or learn how to put systems in place to keep you from being so negatively affected that you end up hurting yourself either physically or emotionally. Once you identify your triggers, take some time to figure out where they stem from.

Do any of these circumstances trigger you?

- Someone rejecting you.
- Someone leaving you (or the threat that they will).
- Helplessness over painful situations.
- Someone discounting or ignoring you.
- Someone being unavailable to you.
- Someone giving you a disapproving look.
- Someone blaming or shaming you.
- Someone being judgmental or critical of you.
- Someone being too busy to make time for you.
- Someone not appearing to be happy to see you.
- Someone coming on to you sexually in a needy way.
- Someone trying to control you.
- Someone being needy or trying to smother you.

mindbodygreen.com

Think back to your childhood to determine why certain things lead you to have emotional responses.

As in Jasmine's case, it is much easier to avoid your emotional triggers when you are aware of what they are. How do your emotional triggers make you feel?

- I get angry.
- I get needy.
- I comply. I become a people-pleaser.
- I shut down and withdraw from the other person.
- I blame someone else for my pain.
- I turn to an addiction – food, drugs, alcohol, sex, porn, shopping, work gambling, and so on.

mindbodygreen.com

Awareness of your emotional triggers will help you to shift your emotional state. You'll be empowered to detach by clearing your mind of all thoughts, breathing to relax and relieve tension in your body, or center yourself by being alert, present, and bringing harmony into yourself.

Reflection... Tony Robbins

Tony Robbins is someone whose story has motivated me from his presence on stage to his everyday life. Tony Robbins teaches us to have an extraordinary life on our terms. He owned his past filled with shortcomings and walked into a bright future filled with greatness. This could not have happened by accident. First, he had to see himself for who he was.

He has passed the idea that 'who you see is who you become' on to hundreds of thousands of people through the years. Now, we know him as an author and profound life coach hosting seminars around the world, teaching people how to find and harness the power within them. The lifestyle he leads now is nothing compared to where he began. He grew up poor as the oldest of three children to a mother with a revolving door of men. He was so poor and hungry that he would walk around the grocery store eating food because his mother couldn't afford to feed them enough. He was teased in school for wearing high water pants because he grew so fast his mother couldn't afford new clothes. Picture a young Tony in high school, catching a city bus two hours each way to work just for a few hours. As a young adult, he forced himself to stay in an unhappy relationship because he needed his companion's half of the bills to keep a roof over his head.

Tony's whole life, he felt caged, from his mother's verbally abusive behavior to him, her many boyfriends, his brothers, and to just barely having his financial needs met. Day after day, he dreamed about what he would do with his life, the man he would become. He left those thoughts as dreams because he didn't have the resources to do anything about them. He was heartbroken seeing others have the life he thought he deserved, thinking life was unfair, like when the girl he loved gave up on him for a man in a limousine. She wanted security; Tony could barely offer her a meal. Having incidents like that occur again and again and again should have made Tony feel like life was beating him up.

Instead, he cultivated determination. He realized the reason he did not have the life he wanted was his fault, and no one else's. He took ownership and decided, "This will change for me no matter what. Finally looking at an empty chair knowing I could not pay my rent, I could not answer my phone because I owed everybody money in town, knowing my electricity was about to be cut off, and hearing this song by Neil Diamond, *'I am I said to no one there and no one heard at all, not even the chair,'* as I stared at an empty chair. I thought, *Wow, that is so true. I wasn't even supporting myself, much less changing the world, much less doing what I was put here to do.*"

A hunger for meaning rose up in Tony. He stopped pointing fingers at others for his shortcomings and failures and changed his life. He stopped regurgitating the excuses of, "it's not my fault, it's my mother's fault for throwing me out," and "things really aren't that bad," and "I'm still young, so it's ok." The day he decided "I AM" much more than the behaviors I'm demonstrating emotionally, physically, financially, and spiritually, his life transformed. He wrote down a list of things he would no longer settle forever again. A life of mere survival. Being in a relationship with someone he didn't love. Being physically out of shape. Anything less than he believed in. Being broke. Hiding and lying to people.

This is the message he has passed on to the world. He changed the way he saw himself by looking through a lens of honesty. He saw the person he wanted to be, the heights he wanted to reach, the people he wanted to guide to greatness. That is who he became. Through books, videos, and seminars, he teaches others the power of showing up. He encourages us that we deserve better in our lives. Our loved ones deserve a better version of who we are as well to empower them to see and realize an elevated level of potential.

Conclusion

Much like Tony, I was not happy with the path that my life was on. The first step to change was owning that I had challenges I needed help in conquering. The second step was to get help to see my way to the other side of a mountain to attain happiness and fulfillment. Identifying my core values led me to look beyond simply trying to make others happy, instead of focusing on a meaningful, intimate relationship with myself on a quest to get to know who I truly was.

How could I be courageous if I don't even know who I was? Learning and dealing with my history cultivated the person I was at the beginning of this journey. Every single happenstance I lived through shaped my life, as well as my view of it. Realizing this, I was able to discover my personality, and the motivations behind my thoughts and actions. The life I was living was more about pleasing others than giving myself a source of fulfillment, which meant I was not living by my own set of core values. Taking an in-depth look at myself, I was able to carve out the fundamental beliefs that meant a lot to me and use those as guiding principles to center my decisions around.

Embarking on a journey of self-discovery and personal development helped me to dig through the layers of who I was. With courage and guidance, I gained awareness of my life's complexities and who I could become. I could not just proclaim that I wanted to be great, then start anew from where I was. First, I needed to learn myself thoroughly, rebuild the pieces that had caused me to misstep in the past, and move forward with purpose and courage.

5

Face Your Fears

> *"One of the greatest discoveries a man makes, one of his great surprises, is to find he can do what he was afraid he couldn't do."*
>
> Henry Ford

A year after I enrolled in college, my father was sentenced to 20 years in prison. This was such an important time in my life, a time when I desperately wanted to have my parents near. My father and I were extremely close, so you can imagine how devastating that was to me. I had never had to navigate a world without him; I felt insecure in the world without my dad's guidance and presence.

Using the strength he'd raised me with, I decided to direct my harnessed energy and emotions into something constructive. I knew he appreciated my concern but did not want me to spend my days worried about him. I accepted that he was gone away, and there was nothing I could do about it. Rather than wallow, I purposefully chose to move forward productively. I could use the lessons he taught me to make him proud! I worked hard and saved my money to purchase my first home at 20-years-old. My dad had always encouraged me to purchase real estate. I decided to honor his absence by manifesting his vision for me. I had to look my fear of the unknown in the face. Making such a huge purchase at such a young age was quite intimidating to do all alone. It felt so good being able to realize something positive during a time that was so difficult. Much like I channeled the pain of my father going to prison into saving to get into real estate, which was something we often spoke about, you too can overcome fear.

It is human nature to avoid what frightens us. Anything that awakens fearful emotions is something that we'd prefer to shy away from. Why is that? Do you want to walk into a situation that you perceive as being potentially harmful or painful, emotionally, or physically? Me neither.

Fear is not an emotion we are born with; it is taught. When a baby goes near a stove, "Get back!" someone will shout and rush over to the baby, whisking them away. "Put that down!" an adult shouts when little ones pick up trash. "NO! Get down from there!" when a little one climbs up a tree or an elevated surface like a counter. Slowly but surely, we are taught to fear places we should not go or things we should not do.

Initially, hiding from fearful experiences seems more like a self-preservation act. We are protecting ourselves from what could go wrong. We do not want to cause ourselves any undue stress, therefore pivoting away from those dangerous things and people seems like the correct action to take. Rarely do we look at fearful situations as tools for growth.

Once you face fear head-on, it seems less scary. The more you do the things that you have associated with fear, the less paralyzing it becomes. A small bit of anxiety subsides each time you tackle a task associated with fear. I have always been deathly afraid of bugs. I don't want anything creeping, crawling, or flying around me despite growing up in rural Atlanta, a place plagued by tiny wildlife. As a result of seeing my reaction to bugs, guess who else is afraid of bugs? My daughter. If a bug gets in the house, we both jump and scream and yell, aimlessly swatting until it is killed, slithers, or flies away. After each encounter with a bug, I think to myself, *it wasn't that scary.*

Perhaps a better example would be performing my TedTalk. I knew to prepare for the speech facing my fear of people becoming intimately aware of my story would present quite a challenge for me. After months of writing the speech, memorizing, and practicing its delivery, showtime was imminent. In the minutes leading up to walking out on stage in front of hundreds of strangers, I exhibited the classic symptoms of fear: sweaty palms, pacing back and forth, dry mouth, the shakes. I utilized the breathing techniques my counselor taught me to calm myself down when I felt anxiety rearing its ugly head. The techniques worked. But do you know what worked better? Doing the thing, I was afraid to do!

Lean Into Fear

When you feel fear, you have two choices: let the fear stop you or feel it and proceed anyway. If letting fear stop you is not an option, there would be no reason for this section. In feeling fear, you are allowing yourself to acknowledge that there is a risk involved. There is nothing wrong with experiencing this reaction as it is a normal emotion. Unabated, however, the fearful thoughts that arise will increase as time passes. You will become increasingly anxious, coming up with more reasons why you should not do "the thing." The more reasons you identify potential risk with failure, the more you will "lean back." In doing so, you are pulling away from "the thing," creating more space and distance until ultimately you decide you will not do it. In that case, fear wins.

Visualize yourself on a ski slope, skis on your feet, poles in your hands. The base of the slope is the goal. How do you start? By pushing off or leaning in toward the base. The closer you get to the goal (base), you pick up speed. But as you increase speed, what is your natural reaction? What did you do in your visualization? Did you pull back to slow down? Or did you lean in to speed up? Your response depends on what you are prepared to do.

If you pulled back, maybe the increase in speed was a reason to slow down because you felt yourself losing control. Perhaps you weren't fully committed to the goal. You knew you wanted to get to the base, but you were ok taking your time. Maybe you were just plain scared about what was ahead of you, the whole experience altogether. If you leaned in, you are ready for something new and adventurous. You aren't necessarily afraid to fall, get back up, and continue skiing to the base. You are prepared to see what lies in wait for you at the bottom.

If fear has paralyzed you from making it to your goal, it's time for you to lean in. Push off and see where the journey will take you. Lean in toward the goal and away from fears of incompetence, lack of credibility, questioning your worthiness or preparation. Stick your feet in the skis, secure your positioning, and go.

Trust That You Will Recover
Nobody likes to fail. Fearing a less than favorable result is one of the key reasons you haven't stepped into your greatness yet. You fear failure. This, again, is a natural feeling. Missing the mark or coming up short is a part of the process. It's a difficult concept to grasp those feelings of shame, frustration, and guilt that can eventually lead to strength and conquering if we allow ourselves to be in the feelings, recognize their presence, then use them to find the lesson in each failure.

You may try to avoid failure, but what is the likelihood of that happening on some level, especially if you are stepping out of your comfort zone or leaning in towards a new goal? If you accept that learning or trying anything new is challenging and you will experience setbacks, you also accept that you will recover from those setbacks. A lesson in failing gracefully will ensure that you don't fail and give up, but rather let the failure set you up for greater success. That is what you do during the recovery period.

Encourage your success by having faith that the roadblocks that have gotten in your way will not hold you back. Adjust your mindset to know that a single failure, or multiple failures, will not keep you chained to losing indefinitely. Success takes effort! Think about these greats who believed they would recover and did.

- Harland David Sanders went bankrupt driving around to 1,009 restaurants begging them to use his Kentucky Fried Chicken recipe. Finally, a restaurant decided to give his recipe a shot agreeing to pay him five cents commission for each piece of chicken sold. Hello KFC!
- Oprah Winfrey was fired from her first news anchor job, citing she was too emotionally invested. She leaned in to create the most-watched TV talk show of all time.
- Iconic wedding dress designer Vera Wang had hopes of making the 1986 Olympic Figure-skating Team. She didn't make the cut, did a career pivot into an editorial seat at *Vogue*. After 15 years, she began designing dresses. The rest is history.

Reflection... Sojourner Truth

The name Sojourner Truth is synonymous with women's and civil rights. Born Isabella Baumfree as an enslaved person in upstate New York in 1797, Truth grew accustomed to the horrible treatment of slaves. Once her Dutch-speaking enslavers passed away, she was sold at an auction block to an English-speaking enslaver. At only 9-years-old, she was beaten incessantly for not understanding her new owners. After changing hands a few times, she landed on a plantation next to the one where her future husband toiled.

Several years after marriage and three children, Truth was promised freedom; her enslaver reneged on the deal. She put in the amount of work she felt was owed to him, then ran away with her youngest child. Luring her back with the promise of pay instead of enslavement, Truth returned only to find that her 5-year-old son had been sold. With the aid of activist Quakers, she filed an official complaint in court. It took months of legal proceedings, but her son was eventually returned to her. He was fragile from abuse and scarred, but he was alive. Her case was the first in which a Black woman successfully challenged a white man in a United States court when she accused him of illegally selling her son.

Can you imagine the fear that accompanied being a Black person formerly enslaved in the early 1800s? Truth was dark-skinned, far from being light enough to pass as white. She endured the full gamut of mistreatment of enslaved people, but when her son was kidnapped, she did not let the fear of what could happen to her prevent her from seeking justice. What an amazing feeling of vindication she must have felt winning her son back! I'm sure she did not think it would end favorably for her. Still, she persisted and leaned in for her desired outcome.

Later in her life she was charged with poisoning and murder; her son left on a whaling ship and disappeared under curious circumstances. Yet, these harrowing situations did not stop her from helping people. Truth went on to be a voice of justice for women and Black people alike. As an abolitionist and speaker, she toured the country demanding equal rights as and for those of her likeness. Even though opponents twisted around and changed the words of her speeches, white men scorned her message, and the very white women she sought to help laughed at her orations, where it came to social reform and activism, fear was no part of Truth's equation. No matter what you are facing, it should not be a part of yours either.

Conclusion

Fear is inevitable when you're living your life courageously. It is important to "do it with courage" versus "doing it scared." When we address fear from a courageous place, we gain the confidence to lean into fear and trust that no matter what happens, we will recover. When we address fear from a place of trepidation, we do not maximize our opportunities because the focus is on removing the uncomfortable feeling.

We don't want to lead a life that will end in regret. There is no point in landing safely at death. You don't get an award for that. Don't dread loving out of fear of rejection. Don't fear sharing ideas that will prove you to be more of an asset to your company out of fear you will be laughed at. Let go of your fearful stance hunched over with your arms folded. Stand up proudly, know who you are and whose you are, walk and speak with confidence, then lean into fear.

Respond to fear with:

- *Understanding.* Fear is meant to keep us safe, not inactive. Use it to make more informed decisions instead of yielding total control.
- *Action.* Some people are quick to take action, but if fear is involved, they won't be. You can still move in the right direction, even in your fear. Take advantage of an intentional action plan that positions you for success. Use the time to educate yourself to examine the situation based on facts versus speculation. Enlist a coach, mentor, or peer to help you define the steps needed to move past fear.
- *Support.* Peer pressure is real. Have you ever been a part of a group that did something scary, but when it came time, you froze? Did you notice that having other members of the group cheering you on or picking at you encouraged you to act? Tell someone what your goal is and what you fear, let them push you to overcome what is holding you back.

6

Pace Yourself for the Journey

"Life is a journey, not a destination."

Ralph Waldo Emerson

When I arrived in my late 20s, I was newly divorced and overjoyed with the single life! After being in an unhealthy relationship for over seven years, freedom was the sweetest taste I could have ever imagined. So many traumatic experiences clouded my future, that seeing so much possibility in front of me, for the first time, was invigorating. This new feeling left me eagerly excited to recreate my life and achieve maximum fulfillment.

I moved at lightning speed with an overwhelming excitement each day. I was so eager to make up for the time that I'd lost and experiences that I so desperately desired. One day I was out shopping and found a new pair of sunglasses that practically spoke my name when I walked past the rack. I tried them on and they looked great; but, I noticed my peripheral vision was impaired. The old Kathi may have been sensible and put them back. Yet, in that moment, I was too busy to think through the purchase. I tried to adjust my vision while walking to the car. However, when I began to drive, it was even harder to see. "I'll be ok," I told myself speeding through life, not stopping to think for a minute that my vision was impaired, and I was possibly putting my life and others' lives in danger.

"I'll be ok," had become somewhat of a mantra that I said to myself. No matter what was going on, I would say, "I'll be ok," to myself and keep pushing. "I'll be ok," is how I survived years of childhood trauma and an abusive relationship. In rushing to get to a specific finish line I had for myself, I didn't stop to think, readjust, or strategize. In this season of my life, I consistently rushed ahead in my thinking, as well as in all of my actions. In any given moment, I had a thousand ideas and worries floating around in my head. Subsequently, my actions were always trying to keep up with my racing, competing, and jumbled thoughts. Forget stopping to smell the roses, I barely even saw them. I had tunnel vision, but in the instance of rushing through life, it was not a good thing.

On this specific day, I suffered my fourth serious car accident in just two years. Every time I looked up, my car insurance was increasing and I found myself at the repair shop fixing a dent. The sheer embarrassment alone should have been a wake-up call. I finally recognized that I was the common denominator and I needed to make some changes within myself. I took a hard look in the mirror acknowledging that I was moving too fast and would have to slow down to make real progress in life.

Being Intentional with Your Actions is Necessary

In my personal life, managing my pace has been one of the most difficult challenges. It typically becomes unbalanced when I am overly excited or anxious about my future. These moments have occurred during times of transition, new opportunities, or unexpected changes. These moments have resulted in me being overly confident or the complete opposite, lacking confidence. In either scenario, my confidence is skewed and God is not at the center of my decisions. Ephesians 5:11 (Message Version) declares, "Don't waste your time on useless work, mere busywork, the barren pursuits of darkness. Expose these things for the sham they are."

One of the conditions that contribute to unclear thinking is being too busy. We are human beings; however, the urge to "do" can take over if we are not intentional with our actions. The unwillingness to delegate tasks or overcommitting ourselves can lead to working harder instead of smarter. Whether we are at work, church, or in a casual setting, when the question of "How are you doing?" is asked, "I'm so busy!" is the typical response. The response is typically followed by a rundown of our most recent list of activities. We live in a world where people relish running around like chickens with their heads cut off.

Sometimes we are genuinely... well, busy. There are work activities, social functions that we absolutely can't miss, family gatherings, and supporting our children in their myriad of events. By saying, "I'm so busy," we are really saying more than, "I have an active lifestyle." We are saying, "I have a lot to do." Instead of prioritizing those things, we are implying, "I am working quickly to get through them with little to no time-saving strategies, so my energy and attention are depleted, and very little is getting accomplished."

Organization is Key to Pace

Being "busy" is not a good thing when you have no plan on how to accomplish the goals at hand. You must pace yourself for the journey ahead. Cramming our schedule full of meetings at work, being under the gun for deadlines, paying bills, and family commitments is a great way to invite stress and anxiety into our lives. You may have been privy to this type of adrenaline rush. So, you think by you pulling yourself in 10,000 directions, you're doing a little or this and a little of that, surely you are fruitfully getting things accomplished.

The truth is, having high levels of activity don't necessarily lead to productivity. When asked how I am doing, I am very conscious to answer, "I am productive." Even if I am not, I am working on being productive and speaking it into existence. There is a difference between being busy and being productive. Being busy is working hard, frantic, and seems to focus on perfectionism. Productivity is goal-oriented work driven by a purpose that is focused on an end result. People who say they are busy, tend to think getting more work done in a set period is the way to go. They chock their schedules full of items that ultimately get moved on to the next day's to-do list. Productive people know they cannot get 40 items done in a day. Instead, they take a less is more approach concentrating on actually seeing tasks through to completion.

Establish A Pace

Pace means to walk at a steady rate. Establishing a pace means you just go and go and go. In rushing to cram as much as possible in your schedule, in addition to not being as productive as you'd like to think you are, you are also shorting yourself on the other end. You will get off pace, which will take away more time.

Have you ever heard of burnout? The term means different things to different people. In general, it is exhausttion in every sense of the word: mentally, physically, and emotionally. Examples of how to recognize when your time is being robbed from being off pace are when you face burnout, anxiety, impatience, constant frustration, inability to say "no" or "yes" as appropriate.

After being inundated with constant demands, burnout can be a strong urge to quit, or not continue with a project, relationship, or job. Anxiety can be a strong sense of uneasiness, often your breathing will be out of sync and your mind will race. Impatience can be a strong urge to move things forward without consideration of the impacting variables. Constant frustration is dissatisfaction with everything and everyone. The inability to say "no" or "yes" as appropriate, is where you are walking around with a pre-ordered response, everything is either "yes" or "no" without consideration or consulting with God.

When you are not pacing yourself towards your purpose – aside from stumbling, tripping, and falling – you are exhausted physically, mentally, and emotionally and most importantly, spiritually. In this realm, you are likely not spending time with God, hearing God, or adhering to His directions. A lot of time is wasted during this period.

On the contrary, when you are pacing yourself for your purpose, you aren't burnt out because you are seeking God in everything that you do, and He is guiding you on when to say "no" and when to say "yes". You can manage or release anxiety, impatience, and frustration from your life. You are trusting God's plans, timing, and each occurrence – whether it feels good or not. In this realm, magic happens – also known as grace and favor. When you are on pace, you can see God in everything; He will provide abundant wisdom, revelations, and resources that will maximize your time.

Beware of Distractions

Productivity-busting habits develop over time. When you are busy, you are doing just that. Typically, this is when you attract people, places, and things that can waste a lot of time. This happens because just being busy does not lend to getting tasks accomplished, but rather doing a little bit of work on many tasks. Every time the phone buzzes...you check it. If your phone rings...you answer it. When a new email comes...you look to see who it is from and may even respond to it. In the long term, distractions can be more damaging. Let's say someone is saving for a house by dedicating $500 a month towards the down payment when a vacation is proposed to them. Going on that vacation could mean spending three months' worth of savings, which not only pushes back the home purchase, but they spend more money in the long run because they are still renting as well. Anytime an interruption comes into their lives, some compulsively respond to it.

Pace Yourself to Win

You may read the title of the chapter "Pace Yourself for the Journey" and instantly envision a real foot race. During a marathon, runners take off and find a steady pace to run. They don't run full speed the entire race. That would be impossible. Even if it were not impossible, going full speed would have them struggling at the end. They conserve their energy so they can comfortably run towards the finish line with a little extra *umph* in their tanks, saving energy reserves for when they need to step it up during the last leg of the race. They are aware of their environments, aware of their bodies, and have total mind control for hours ahead.

Just like marathon runners pace themselves, we must do the same in this race of life. We cannot allow ourselves to get so overwhelmed that we want to give up. Through prayer and connection to God, we can seek His help and ask that He send reinforcements when necessary; but we must still do our part to ensure we are journeying forward smartly.

There are times when you can't help that some-thing comes at you at the last minute. You're up late burning the midnight oil finishing a project, and that's exactly what you do. The next day, you feel amazingly accomplished, yet, you are exhausted throughout the rest of the day, and the attention you pay to the tasks of that day wane because of how tired you are.

Pacing yourself for the win means this is an exception, not the norm. It means to improve your personal productivity, you must slow down a little. You didn't get where you are by rushing and hurrying along life's path. When goals have a specific due date, don't say, "I'm going to have this finished by May 1st," without a way to ensure that it gets done. Map out a plan-of-action. Being too ambitious for your own good will, again, only hurt you in the long run. When you realize it's April 15th, and you have not dedicated the amount of time and resources to the project to get it done, your self-esteem will take a significant blow. This could lead to you giving up on the project altogether.

Reflection... Michael Phelps

Michael Phelps is the most decorated Olympian in any sport boasting 28 medals. Sure, his stature has something to do with his phenomenal abilities. Standing at 6'4", he has the wingspan of a person who stands 6'8". His diet and routine also have something to do with his substantial wins. During a 2008 Beijing Summer Olympics interview with NBC, he discussed consuming 12,000 calories per day to fuel his five-hour, six-days-per-week training leading up to the games. But that is not pace, that was routine.

As the youngest of three children, he became very close to his mother and sisters when his parents divorced at age 9. Their sibling bond coaxed him to join the swim team because his older sisters were both partaking in the sport. At 7, and terrified to put his head underwater, Michael's coaches allowed him to float on his back. Is it any surprise that he mastered the backstroke first? His eldest sister even tried out for the 1996 Olympic swim team but was unable to compete due to injuries.

Watching those 1996 Olympic Games ignited a desire in him to become a champion. Michael's talents began to truly shine by training with his coach, Bob Bowman, at North Baltimore Aquatic Club at the Meadowbrook Aquatic and Fitness Center. That is also where pacing for his long journey to success began to take form. Through an intense training regime and naturally armed with a fierce sense of competition, Michael and his trainer worked tirelessly six days a week to align him with his goal of becoming an Olympic swimmer. By 1999, he'd made the U.S. National B Team. At the age of 15, at the 2000 Olympic Games, he became the youngest American male swimmer to compete at the Games in 68 years. Amazingly, in 2001, Michael set the world record in the 200-meter butterfly, becoming the youngest male swimmer in history (at 15 years and 9 months) to ever set a world swimming record.

Let's pause here for a minute. He became the youngest male swimmer in history to *ever* set a world swimming record. Think about the enormity of that statement. Do you think this could have happened if he had not found a pace early on in his career? I think it's highly unlikely. By pacing himself with a workout, eating, and swimming regimen, and arming himself with a vision for success, Michael was able to chip away at the unlikelihood that his dreams would come true. Knowing what grueling tasks lay ahead, he prepared himself with the mindset that going to the Olympics was a journey, not just a quick trip.

Conclusion

In conclusion, lacking pace – moving too fast – can cause you to misstep and miss out on the favor of God. Don't mistake motion for productivity. Recognize that God wants us to be balanced physically, mentally, emotionally, and spiritually. Awareness of your pace is a key aspect of monitoring and managing it. If you find yourself lacking pace, **STOP. BREATHE. RESET.** You do not have to conform to the expectations of everyone else, that job, that project, that to-do list will always be there. Your opportune moments of destiny are limited – keep yourself at a pace so that you can seize them.

How can you pace yourself?
- *Be content.* Paul says this about contentment in Philippians 4:12: "I have learned the secret of being content in any and every situation" (NIV). Being content doesn't mean you don't want to grow or aspire to do anything great. It means you understand success is a process, and just because you reach that shiny pinnacle of success that you think will make you happy, doesn't mean that it will.
- *Obey the fourth commandment.* Take a day off. When you are super busy, you feel like you have to keep working on getting it all done. Rather than feel accomplished, you just feel overworked. Take that time off to revive your mind, refresh your soul, and reinvigorate your spirit. When you get back to work, the quality of the work you do will be leaps and bounds above the laborious energy you had on day 6 of the week.
- *Pause and pray before moving forward.* Ask, "God, what do you want me to do in this instance?" This

will help you to slow down and gain perspective. Perspective is what you need to make wise decisions.
- *Learn to say "no."* You simply cannot make every baby shower, every PTA meeting, every birthday party, and every family reunion. Prioritize which events require your presence versus those you can follow-up with later, or not.
- *Me time?* Yes, me time! Indulge in self-care activities such as going to the movies alone, or out for a cup of ice cream. Plan a weekend staycation in the city if you don't want to fork up thousands of dollars for an international trip. Find a way to be at peace alone.
- *Aromatherapy.* Think about the last time you walked into a spa or a really swanky hotel. As soon as you hit the door you were met with a signature scent of some kind. What did it do to you? Chances are, it relaxed you. You can bring this feeling of calm to your day-to-day life with natural oils in the shower or plug-ins around your home. When you step in after a long, hectic, busy day, you'll be met with a scent to carry you away.

Exercise: Create a Success Statement to manage your Pace

What does success look like for you? Often our pace is inconsistent because we are not clear on where we are going. Success will look different depending upon what season of your life you are in. Close your eyes and imagine yourself fulfilled, committed, joyful, and energized about life. Now write a powerful statement to describe a few objectives that would be in place to achieve this feeling.

For example, maybe success is being physically healthy. One of your objectives could state, I AM healthy and practicing a healthy diet with a consistent workout plan. Be realistic. If another one of your success factors is better management of your finances, having your healthy meals catered daily will not be a part of your plan. Bold, specific, and congruent objectives will increase your motivation, accountability, and consistency.

SECTION THREE

Excited for the Future

7

Create a Compelling Vision

"What you focus on grows, what you think about expands, and what you dwell upon determines your destiny."

Robin S. Sharma

"How did I get here?" I asked myself. Standing in the mirror, I was 20 pounds heavier than when I started my weight loss journey. Going through a divorce was a challenging time for me. I'd heard over and over being divorced was like mourning a death. The full weight of that statement did not strike me until it was all said and done. I was exactly where I did not want to be, a divorced single parent. I poured my focus into the gym. With a lot of hard work and discipline, I had gotten in the best shape of my life. Having a new goal to put energy into helped me to look and feel good. Then, there I was after gaining back all the weight I'd lost and then some. The good news is, I had lost the weight before, and I knew I could do it again!

Recently, I was at the gym trying a new weight-lifting position that heavily relied on abs for strength. My abs are far from the strongest muscles in my body, so to say the exercise was challenging is an understatement. Each time I attempted the exercise, my mind would wander to the lack of strength that I had, which only threw off my form. My coach instructed me to focus on the weight with my eyes, and my body would follow. Sure, enough, this worked. Just as in everyday life, our minds wander, focusing our attention and energy on the issues and challenges we are facing. However, when we instead focus on the path toward the solutions, we can make progress.

Let me share with you a piece of my journey that required vision to see it to the end. My educational journey started in Atlanta, then abruptly shifted to Denver in 5th grade for middle school. The same scenario repeated itself when I was relocated to Indianapolis for most of high school. I had to make new friends so often in my formative years that I placed a higher value on friendships and personal connections than my studies. For the most part, I was a good student, but I had anger issues from childhood trauma and was a distracted student who struggled with fitting in. As a result, I ended up in physical altercations routinely. These types of problems continued until I was expelled from high school.

During my senior year of high school, I was very eager to learn how to drive, but my mother was scared to teach me. So, I went back to Atlanta to learn and finish high school. Yes, learning how to drive and having a car was so serious to me that I relocated to do it, but moving back in with my dad wasn't as easy as I thought it would be. I'd lived with my mother for so many years, that being with under his authority and listening to him proved to be quite a task. This mindset, coupled with the childhood trauma of being molested, shuffling around, and my parents' unwillingness to accept what had happened, caused me to rebel. My first real act of rebellion? Moving out on my own at the age of 16.

Even though I was rebelling at home, I still had a vision of graduating. I was determined not to let anything keep me from getting that piece of paper. For me to make ends meet, I transferred to an open campus to finish high school, where I could juggle attending for a few hours in the morning with my two full-time jobs. I ended up graduating early, but at 17 in my own apartment and supporting myself, I was really living an adult life. I learned real quick what sacrifice was. Hot dogs and potato chips were my daily meal with a splurge being a kid's meal from Chick-Fil-A. The mental shift came for me when I realized how much life I was missing with the new job I acquired. Sure, at 18, I was making $30,000 a year, but I was working 8-to-1 then 5-to-9. Since the job was so far away from my apartment, I had to remain close by during my four-hour break. I missed birthday parties, family reunions, spending time with my loved ones and getting rest. I decided getting a high school diploma wasn't enough for me. I wanted a career.

After completing my bachelor's degree, I immediately enrolled to earn my master's. By this point, my vision of finishing high school grew to push myself to the ultimate finish line: a doctorate. Half-way through the master's program, I got pregnant with my daughter. A year after having her, I became laser-focused. Making a living was about more than myself at that point, it was also about establishing a quality of life for my daughter. I also knew that it was going to become harder and harder to succeed the older she got. Being a new wife and new mom, time was hard to come by.

After the divorce, I decided to go back for my doctorate degree. Unlike the other degrees and high school, finishing early was not in my cards. It took me over seven years to complete. Through it all, the life challenges, the struggles, and the sacrifices, I held tight to the future I saw for myself. Dr. Kathi Middleton walked across the stage, realizing a dream that took well over a decade to finish.

Every one of us was created for a unique purpose and has a distinct path to travel on to be successful, we must follow that path with a distinct focus. Whether we were created to be doctors, teachers, musicians, therapists, or artists, the challenge that many of us of face is being distracted along the journey to our purpose. Life will present opportunities and blessings that energize us and catapult us to accomplish great things. While on the journey, life will also present curve balls that can take us off the course away from our purpose and test whether we are truly committed to that purpose.

> "Imagination is more important than knowledge. For knowledge is limited, whereas imagination embraces the entire world, stimulating progress, giving birth to evolution."
>
> Albert Einstein

Principles of Focus

You may already know what your purpose is. You may even be headed in the direction of breathing life into the very things that will help you fulfill your purpose. But it is also possible that you lack focus. Your mind darts from one thing to another. That's natural because life throws unexpected challenges at us, like me bumping heads with my dad to the point where I felt I had to move out. Without having a focus on what you want to accomplish, it is hard to chip away at it long enough to see it to fruition. This can be incredibly frustrating and, in the long run, cause you to give up hope on ever feeling that sense of fulfillment that you crave.

This makes the power of focus so critical. Being taken off course by shiny new possibilities or broken situations that will inevitably pop up while you are on your path will make it impossible to finish what you started. Helen Keller could have easily given up her activism for the handicapped when she was attacked through slander. Many people insinuated her condition as a blind and deaf person was caused by a venereal disease implying it was of her own doing. She wasn't going to let that stop her, however. She had a vision that compelled her to drive forward.

Focus on Your Priorities

Your mind is your greatest asset; however, it can be your greatest detriment without proper focus. When we focus our minds on what we want to achieve, opposed to the things that are getting in the way, we create space, energy, and alignment to attract what we need. Motivational speaker Zig Ziglar said, "Lack of direction, not lack of time is the problem. We all have 24 hours in a day."

Plan your days ahead. Each night map out how you want the following day to go. Without having a clear goal for what needs to be accomplished the next day, you will end up wasting precious time that you cannot reclaim. If you need to, write it all out on a notepad or in the note app on your phone. The goal is to give yourself minute directions that will push you toward your major goals. Whether it is something as small as writing a blog or pulling your credit history to craft a household budget, write a list with the allotted time you want to devote to each task. Seeing them written down will help to ensure things get done.

Focus on your Desired Results

Say you have a goal that will take a year to accomplish, so what? The time will pass by anyway. If you go into it conscious of how long it will take, you will be less discouraged as the days turn into weeks, and weeks turn into months. You will remember this is a part of the process. I knew going into the doctorate program that it was going to take me about four years. I was fully prepared for that length of time to pass, but when it took longer, I focused on the end goal: my desired result.

Using the household budget from *Focus on Your Priorities* above, let's use the example of purchasing a home. If you only focus on what you are giving up in order to save for the down payment on that home, you will make yourself miserable and talk yourself out of sticking to your plan. However, if you imagine yourself on the porch of a new home, having a movie night with your family inside a spacious living room, or standing outside watering your grass, it will help you to get excited about what lies ahead. Keep the end goal fresh in your mind. Remind yourself why this goal means so much to you and your family.

Leverage Your Strengths and Acknowledge Your Weaknesses

People become successful by understanding what they are good at and acknowledging what they are not good at. Each one of us has strengths and each one of us has weaknesses. If your goal is directly related to a strength or proficiency you can develop over time, great! If not, figure out a way to leverage your strengths to help propel yourself into the direction of your goal. Then identify your weaknesses and acknowledge them. We all have areas we are less proficient in. These are the areas where you will want to seek support. Depending on the importance of the skill in the situation, you may want to find the most competent, talented, organized person you can outsource it to.

There are 24 hours in a day. It's important to maximize your time by doing what you do well and allowing others to do what they do well. There is no harm in admitting that you need help in certain areas. It is not only a wise move, but it will also save you money down the road. This principle is also in line with eliminating tasks that don't add value. Why squander useful hours or days trying to complete a task you know will be exceptionally challenging for you? Don't. Instead, find someone who can do it with ease while you focus on performing to your strengths.

Focus on Embodying and Communicating Your Vision

"Good leaders must communicate vision clearly, creatively, and continually. However, the vision doesn't come alive until the leader models it," says John C. Maxwell. Don't get stuck trying to force others to see your vision. Your vision will not sweep through the hearts of those who hear about it with passion and fervor. That job is for your heart.

Nothing will motivate you like a clear and concise vision. It can be taxing to describe your vision to others as it is in your mind. When they do get it, it fuels you to keep going. In Helen Keller's instance, the numerous awards she received, including the Theodore Roosevelt Distinguished Service Medal in 1936, the Presidential Medal of Freedom in 1964, and election to the Women's Hall of Fame in 1965 let her know that the vision was getting across.

If you do struggle with helping others see or understand your vision. You can inspire them to capture a glimpse of it with a few quick steps:

- *Connect.* Facts are dry and boring. There is a story behind each vision, a group that you want to reach and inspire. When explaining your vision to others, learn to connect with their emotions. If you can pull at their heartstrings, then you have a better chance of them viewing your goals through the same passion that drives you.
- *Simplify the message.* One of the greatest speeches to go down in the annals of history is the Gettysburg Address; yet, Abraham Lincoln only spoke for three minutes. It's not what you say, it's the delivery that you give. Cut down your vision into a powerful 60-90 second elevator pitch. The simpler it is, the better chance you have of your audience understanding and remembering it.
- *Honor the process.* The longer your vision needs to take shape, the more milestones you will cross to get there. Celebrate each victory as this gives you

multiple opportunities to reinforce your vision. Each defeat should be evaluated, offering a change, of course, where necessary.

- *Embody the vision.* People need a vision they can connect with, which can be done by harnessing a great storytelling approach. Your energy is contagious. If you are timid about your vision, that will not yield a great deal of support. But if you are burning with a desire to see it to the end, they will be attracted to help fan your flame.
- *Call to action.* Put steps in place to make your vision a reality. If you need help, enlist others who have done it and can guide you or answer questions along the way. You should not expect others to fully get your vision. Rather, you have the responsibility of turning it from a dream into something they can see, feel, and believe in... reality.

Reflection... Hellen Keller

My pastor gave a message that resonated with me using Proverbs 29:18 that says, "Where there is no vision, the people are unrestrained." They can't focus, can't reach their goal, can't follow their dream. An older translation says, "Without vision, the people perish."

Think about having the use of your senses for a minute. Being able to see, hear, and feel. How much of your day involves sight and hearing? Now, can you imagine not being able to do either? Visualize this story as you read it.

Hellen Keller triumphed over blindness and deafness. Struck with a disease that left her blind and deaf at the tender age of 19 months, she was forced to learn objects by touch and associate them with drawings inside of the palm of her hand. By age 14, she'd learned how to speak and read lips by placing her fingers to the speaker's mouth and throat. Close your eyes, put one hand on your lips and another on your throat and say, "Hello. How are you?" Now, use one hand to make hand signals or shapes in the other. Could you handle a world communicating in that way?

After earning her degree cum laude, at 24 in 1904, Keller began to write for women's magazines about blindness. Due to her approach to acquiring skills never approached by any similarly disabled person, there was a great deal of interest in the life she chronicled in the six books she wrote. She was determined to improve the way those who were deaf and blind were treated, including having many removed from asylums. By 1937, she spearheaded deaf and blind commissions in 30 states.

Her life story became a Broadway play, TV drama, and award-winning film, The Miracle Worker. You see, she wasn't doing it for the numerous awards she received, she wanted to be the voice and sight for the deaf and blind. Hellen Keller was determined to communicate and refused to allow any impediment, distraction, or frustration to prevent her from achieving her goal, as well as helping others to have an open avenue for communication. By bringing awareness to her disabilities, she was able to educate those who cared for their loved ones with the same disabilities, as well as beginning a legacy to educate the general public. She was focused on doing just that and spent her life living up to her vision.

While this is an extreme example, it should reinforce that nothing is impossible. We are all capable of greatness, we need only to search within ourselves for the belief that we can and the tenacity that we will.

Conclusion

When you decide to push yourself outside of your comfort zone to accomplish greatness, your vision will grow, and creative ideas will begin to pour in. When you decide to have the courage to be great, you commit to growth. If I may quote John Maxwell, "If we are growing, we are always going to be outside our comfort zone." Your excitement, passion, and zeal for a purpose will also attract an abundance of new people and opportunities. If not managed appropriately, these things can become a distraction to you. In addition to the blessings, challenges will be inevitable. When it seems like every possible issue is arising to throw you off course, what you do next will determine whether you reach your destination of purpose.

The answer lies in two simple steps. The first is to get laser-focused on where you are going and recognize who has called you to that place. There is not one thing that God gives you the vision for without equipping you with the resources to accomplish it. God's strength is made perfect in our weakness. When we are weak and unequipped, God can do His best work inside of us. God insists on getting the glory, and in our weakness, we are forced to rely on Him for everything.

The second step in reaching our destination of purpose is to renew and manage our energy. Energy is the most valuable resource on the planet. When we are energized and excited about our vision, an influx of people, opportunities, and circumstances will present themselves. It is important to discern the distractions that would take energy away from your vision quickly. Each of us has a limited supply of energy. When we attempt to water too many plants, none of them receive enough nourishment to grow. It is okay to be stingy with your energy and time. Do what you must do now so that you can do what you want to do later. Don't expect people to understand what it takes to accomplish your goals. When God gives you a vision, He gives this to you and you alone. Be okay with being misunderstood while you are building and executing your vision. When you have finished building, your fruits will benefit everyone connected to you, and it will be worthwhile. Is it more important for you to complete your goal, or are you most concerned with being liked or valuable? Great men are often despised and misunderstood in seasons of focus.

How can you realize a compelling vision for your life? By putting it in writing. You are shaping your destiny with each decision you make, and by putting your vision in writing, you are creating a visual that will help to work for you. Much like the vision, I saw of myself walking across the stage as Dr. Kathi Middleton, I had to map out the steps and revisit my goal to achieve my mission. Below are two simple steps to guide your compelling vision.

Exercise: Create a Personal Vision Statement & Track How You are Spending Your Time

1. Outline a compelling vision statement for your life.

2. Track how your time is spent each day for a week. Then start by creating a daily To-Do List of Your Top 5 Priorities and a To-Done List of what you accomplished, including bonus items.

Creating a compelling vision will motivate you to achieve your goals. Outlining your tasks will help you stay focused and avoid distractions. Acknowledging and taking time to celebrate the items you complete will give you the momentum to finish.

8

Build a Healthy Community

"If you want to go fast, go alone. If you want to go far, go together."

African Proverb

Having been raised in a rural area where our neighbors were miles down the road, I was shocked the first time a neighbor stopped by my apartment for sugar. I will never forget this experience because it felt so foreign to me. I was raised to be self-sufficient and do what is necessary for your family. However, when you decide to go beyond personal success and achieve greatness you need a team of people to help you get there and hold you up. You also need people you can pour into to keep growing, by giving back to others.

Throughout school, we are on a mission to be the most popular. The years spent in middle school and high school find most of us trying to collect friends like youngsters collect eggs in an Easter basket. We break off into social groups of stereotypical significance, but still want others to know, acknowledge, and validate our existence. At those ages, we don't know anything about quality over quantity, insisting that whoever has the most signatures in their yearbook is the winner of the friend race. We are confident that the number of friends we have plays into our coolness factor.

Enter social media, "How many friends do you have on Facebook?" In all honesty, that figure is grossly inflated as at least one-third of those people are from high school or college; people we barely know and probably only accepted their request because we had so many friends in common, so we feel we must know of them.

As age lends its way to wisdom, we realize the adage of quality over quantity really is plausible. We appreciate having others in our corner who encourage and support us. Most of us are happy with a handful of friends who we know we can rely on rather than 100 friends who just know us in passing.

Cultivating community means finding those who you can truly count on, who can also count on you. Part of embracing people as individuals, regardless of their background, is releasing racial bias. This will help you eliminate a significant amount of negative tension between you and those who you are forced to spend time with. Even co-workers can become an extended family if you allow yourself to look beyond race and culture to see them as people while finding similar interests and beliefs between you.

When you find those who are like-minded to form your newly crafted mental image of the community, do so with exuberance. Forget the small talk and dive into conversations that enliven you both. Let your passions excite and connect you! Believe that God is connecting you for a reason. "When we consider the fact that we are all mere human beings, the possibilities of connections are endless. I believe that you can make an indelible impact among the greatest and the least of these by simply sparking up a conversation as if you were picking up where you left off with an old friend," Rebecca Davis said.

Cultivating Community

Communities are helpful for us because they provide support from the daily stresses, struggles, and chaos of modern life. Having others close to your mind and heart is a basic human need. In the book *The Power of Meaning: Crafting a Life That Matters* by Emily Esfahani Smith, one of the four pillars upon which meaning rests is belonging. Without a sense of belonging, your life would lose its meaning. As important as food and shelter, the feeling that we belong makes it easier to face life's wins and losses. Human connection is natural; it makes us feel happy and secure.

Whether we realize it or not, having a sense of community affects us in many ways, personally, socially, and in business. Once you have established common ground with others, it enables you to communicate with them effectively in a way that brings you closer to them. There are many circumstances in which you may find yourself with the opportunity or social obligation to start a conversation with someone you don't know. Work events, social gatherings, or standing in line at the bank, puts you in situations with others who you don't know. Finding common ground helps to build connectivity through which a friendship can build.

The beauty of establishing a community blooms when being thrust in these types of environments. It showcases your ability to partner and collaborate with diverse individuals. We live in a world where we can access information from all across the globe. In the same token, we are also very likely to work around and befriend people from other backgrounds. Why would anyone think they can cultivate a strong, stable community without contrasting backgrounds and mindsets? Diversity does not mean disagreement; it merely implies comparing values or thought processes. If you open yourself to a varied group of people, you are also enriching your community, as well as opportunities for personal development. Finding common ground between you will be the basis for practicing love and understanding within that community.

By embracing the community, you will create new and transformative perspectives to promote:

- *Access to a diverse range of experiences and expertise.* Opening up means not just being satisfied with what you learn from TV and media, but thoroughly learning other cultures by exposing yourself to them. We should also appreciate that there are things about our own cultures that others want to understand. Additionally, in the workforce, there are so many different disciplines that the information you could learn is baffling. Crossovers of unique skills, experiences, and talents are what leads to innovation. Generating exciting, out of the box ideas is easy when there is a wellspring of collaborative creativity.
- *Support.* Whether we choose to admit it or not, there are hard times in life. Going through them alone is very difficult. Having a community, on the other hand, will offer you the support that you need. Why? Because you will have the opportunity to see your trials through the experience of others who have gone through it themselves or know someone who has.
- *Motivation.* Who doesn't want someone in their corner? Doesn't it feel good to make a goal, strive for that goal, and have people rooting you along? Think about your favorite sports team. As they get closer and closer to scoring, the crowd does what? Gets louder, rowdier. The team thrives on hearing the cheers that motivate them to the end goal. Your community wants to see you win, sometimes even more than you want to see yourself win.

Managing Boundaries

I used to be overly nice. I had no regard for my feelings, my heart, or my resources. I attracted people who consistently wanted to extract from me without ever depositing anything of substance in return. I was loyal to my detriment. One day God showed me that I did not respect my time or energy. He showed me that if I continued to haphazardly give the best things away, I wouldn't be able to accomplish the things that He had set out for me to do. While I was allowing everyone to take advantage of me, I couldn't tap into my real potential. I had even convinced myself that my only purpose was to enable everyone else's purposes. Then God showed me that there were things He wanted me to do for Him. I had to become my own coach to take the steps necessary to implement these things.

Recognize the takers. There are three types of interactions between people: givers, matchers, and takers. Givers do just that, give. They are generous with their spirit and behavior. They encourage you as much as they can, while you come out more on top of the relationship than they do. The matcher gives and takes in equal portions. These people realize that if they give and give, they will get burnt out, so they look for symbiotic behavior in their relationships. On the opposite end of the spectrum from the givers are takers; they bring the most detrimental type of relationship. Takers serve themselves. They often feel that everything is a competition, so they self-promote and put their interests above those of others. Takers don't care about reciprocity, they only care about "me," "my," and "I."

Manage your energy. Dealing with people who take the wind out of your sails can be extremely draining. Going a step further, these relationships are known as toxic relationships. Insults and criticism are five times more impactful than compliments or other types of positive communication. Fearing isolation, because we desire a sense of belonging, will keep us around people who are emotional vampires much longer than we should be. They continuously try to control you and your opinions of other situations and people, while thrusting themselves in situations that lack quick, plausible solutions.

Recognize the relationship for what it is. Have you ever been in a relationship where just being around that person or talking to them consistently brought you down? When you saw them coming, or their name show up on your caller ID, you instantly got a pit in the bottom of your stomach? When you took a step back, what happened? Things got better, didn't they? Don't allow others to dictate the type of day you have. Manage your time and energy by decreasing the contact you have with them. When they begin traveling down a rabbit hole, change the topic to something more mentally healthy. Elevate your vibration by having a positive reaction to their conversation, rather than granting them excitement from seeing you down as well. They won't protect your energy, but you have to because it translates to every other aspect of your life.

Embrace Different Types of Relationships

In T.D. Jakes' book, *Destiny*, he discusses three types of people who are important through your journey: they are confidants, constituents, and comrades. Confidants are going to be the least of the three. This group really has a heart for you, they are excited about your successes and feel the pain of your failures. No matter what is going on in your world, they will make time for you without ever spilling the information you share with them. Constituents don't necessarily support you as a person, but they support your interests. They will not burden themselves with your secrets and life's goals, but overall, you can count on them to rally around something they believe in. Comrades support you! They will fight tooth and nail for you against your enemies. Just like constituents, they aren't intimately involved in your growth as a person, but they will not walk away from your relationship. Each of them is unique and different; however, you must never mistake one for the other. He also discusses that each type of person is necessary to achieve your destiny.

Embrace Different Communities

Be wary of restricting yourself solely to peers with whom you are already familiar and share a history. There is so much more to gain from groups that have diverse backgrounds, education, and life experiences. As you go about your day-to-day life, take a closer look at the people you interact with, including church groups, co-workers, old college classmates, and hobby groups. Each one of these circles has a common thread that connects them; however, there are far more differences between them. Different points-of-view can serve to enlighten you by pointing out thought processes that you have not yet considered. This can help to make you a more well-rounded individual and will come in handy when dealing with people from diverse backgrounds in obligatory settings, such as work.

You can enrich your life by seeking out others. Just as you can enhance someone's life, others can do the same to yours. A network complete with those who have been where you have to go is a win-win for your career. They are often happy to impart wisdom to you because sharing gives them a sense of fulfillment. It is a symbiotic relationship where you can grow as a person and as a professional. You need three such people in your life: a coach, mentor, and sponsor. Coaches train you, mentors guide you, and sponsors promote you.

Conclusion

Sometimes, we undervalue the POWER OF PEOPLE. Everything that God does here on Earth is done through people. Your network is your net worth. Be inspired. Learn and sow into others, which doesn't require money, and allow your faith to be renewed by what God is doing for your neighbor. If your neighbor is being blessed, that means God is in the neighborhood, and YOU'RE NEXT!

9

Commit to Continuous Growth

As we go through life, we always have new experiences that impact the way we see our world. It's essential to not only embrace the changes in the world but our evolution as a person. Evolution is a part of your conscious awakening into who you desire to be. You realize that the pain you experienced is meant to be learned from then released. Each painful memory, failure, and feeling of anxiety has taken place for you to grow from.

Begin with embracing your past. Only you know exactly what you've been through and exactly who hurt you, and how these negative experiences took place. Dig deep into who you were when those life-changing events happened, parallel that with who you are today. What do you need to make peace with? Who do you need to make peace with? What events do you need to look at with a different lens? Are you ready to embrace your past with the affectionate view that it made you who you are? Embrace it, then put it back in its place. Now let's move on.

In removing bias and your limiting beliefs, you should look at yourself with the same adoration as a mother with a child, or Christ and the church. Nothing is stopping you from moving up into a new position, getting a new job, retiring your debt, or traveling the world except you. "But…" don't begin to conjure up excuses to give someone else power. You are fully capable of making adjustments in your life to see the results you seek. You cannot change the color of your skin or what you look like, nor will you be able to change the world's opinion of you to a certain degree. You can, however, live your truth authentically and surround yourself with cheerleaders who will crush your limiting beliefs even when you don't dare to do it yourself.

Own the person you are at this exact moment. Sure, there are things you want to change about yourself. Everyone has attributes they find lackluster. If you want to gain weight, acknowledge that you are not where you want to be, and research ways to gain the muscle or pounds you desire. If you are unhappy with your skin, acknowledge that there are treatments to get and better eating habits that will have your skin glowing! If you are shy, recognize that being around others makes you feel a certain way and begin taking steps to speak out more when in small groups or research networking events to attend. The only way to positively adjust who and where you are is to own who you are first.

Once you own who you are, you will learn what makes you tick. You will embrace your authenticity and put boundaries in place to protect that energy. You will also find yourself interacting more with others who reflect or encourage that same energy. This level of growth is one that is ever-changing as your station in life changes. Different characteristics will be admirable to you as your focus shifts and expands. Own whatever shortcomings and roadblocks come your way as they will mold you into a better version of yourself.

As you grow, don't allow new limiting beliefs to form or resurface. If limiting beliefs try to rear their ugly head, face them head-on. You are now equipped with the tools to lean in to face your fears so that you can live life courageously on your own terms. Do it! Don't let your dreams and goals succumb to anxieties. You are the CEO of your life.

Be prepared for the journey ahead to be a significant one. Just as Barack Obama didn't wake up in the Oval Office one day after he decided he wanted to be president, you can't make a declaration, snap your fingers, and expect to see immediate results. Things take time, growth takes time. Be aware of the steps you need to take, map out a plan, then put that plan into action. It's not going to happen to tomorrow, but your success is waiting for you at the base of the slope.

Before you can go anywhere, you have to have the right mindset to travel. The difference between winners and losers is winners know the journey will be long and are prepared to jump over and walk around what pops up in their paths, while losers stand at the first hurdle, afraid to jump, wondering who put the hurdle there in the first place. Holding on to the vision of accomplishing your goals is what can be used to fuel your journey. Reflect on the feeling of success you anticipate having. How will you feel? What will you say? Who will you tell? How will you celebrate? Hold these visions in your heart and mind as you recruit a team of people to support you along the way.

That team of people will be your community. Your community consists of family, friends, classmates, coaches, sponsors, co-workers, and haters. Yes, even haters; they will give you the push you need to prove them wrong. Don't limit your associations because others don't look like you or share your exact beliefs. Interacting with those different than yourself will do nothing short of expanding and opening your mind.

Live your life, courageously! It is yours and yours alone. You only get one life!

Keep in Touch!

www.kathimiddleton.com

All Social Media: @dr.kathimiddleton

www.ingramcontent.com/pod-product-compliance
Lightning Source LLC
Chambersburg PA
CBHW032049090426
42744CB00004B/136